A NATIONAL SE

Also by Alan Plowright

Plowright Follows Wainwright
Hot-Foot Through The Highlands
A Glimpse of Yorkshire
Another Glimpse of Yorkshire
Land's End to John O'Groats – In Fifteen Years!
Blind Jack
Rock Valley and Oddicroft Lane Recollections *
Memories of Tin Box Making in Mansfield and Sutton   *
John Henry's Walk
In The Footsteps of Stevenson
John Henry's Journeys

*

Compiled in conjunction with Alan Atkins

A NATIONAL SERVICEMAN'S LOT

An account of two years spent in the RAF on
a rite of passage from 1957 to 1959

Alan Plowright

Moorfield Press

First published in Great Britain
by
Moorfield Press 2013
Copyright © Alan Plowright 2013

Page layout by
Highlight Type Bureau Ltd. Bradford, West Yorkshire
Printed in England by
Inprint+ Design Ltd, Bradford, West Yorkshire

A CIP catalogue record for this book is available
from the British Library

ISBN 9780956392916

The moral right of the author has been asserted

Cover design: John W. Holroyd
Colour photographs: Alan Plowright

Contents

Acknowledgements   vi
Foreword   vii
Introduction   viii
Photograph of the author   x

1   Ministry of Labour and National
    Service demand my services.
    Induction at RAF Cardington   1

2   'Square-bashing' at RAF Bridgnorth   7

3   Trade Training at RAF Kirkham   25

4   Joining 34 Fighter Squadron at   36
    RAF Tangmere

5   History of RAF Tangmere, including
    the High Speed Flight, the Schneider
    Trophy and the Suez Crisis   44

6   Life on 65 Fighter Squadron at RAF
    Duxford, including the Jordan Crisis,
    the EOKA Campaign in Cyprus and
    the Munich Air Crash   56

7   History of RAF Duxford, including
    The Battle of Britain and Sir Douglas
    Bader   98

8   Duxford Aerodrome today - Home to
    the Imperial War Museum Duxford   134

    Afterword   149

    Index   152

Acknowledgements

My sincere thanks to the following:

W. R. Mitchell for the Foreword

John W. Holroyd for the cover design

Brian Richardson for proof reading the manuscript and supplying information regarding our service at RAF Duxford

The Old Dux Association

Jim Garlinge, Vice Chairman of the Old Dux Association for providing advice and photographs

The Imperial War Museum, London for providing images of Duxford, various RAF stations and other situations

For the use of 'Britain's Small Wars' copyright material concerning 'The Night the Naafi Blew Up' by David Carter

Foreword
by W. R. Mitchell M.B.E.

'Having spent a compulsory two years of my life on Royal Naval air stations in England Scotland and Ireland, I was keen to read Alan's experiences of the life of a National Serviceman in the RAF. We both experienced life with the drone of aircraft in our ears. A native of Mansfield, Alan worked - before and after his call-up for RAF service - for the Metal Box Company, then for Ranks Hovis McDougall. His leisure time comprises walking, photography and writing. They still give him pleasure.

Alan has found much satisfaction in recalling his immediate post-wartime days. Not content simply to look back on his National Service in the 1950's, when the sky held squadrons of Hawker Hunters, he gives us dual pleasure - one man's insight into the RAF, related via some interesting tales. He had eight weeks of 'square bashing' at RAF Bridgnorth, terrorised by fearsome drill instructors. They 'licked him into shape.' He survived this onslaught and became an airframe mechanic, with trade training at RAF Kirkham, near Preston.

In his book - *A National Serviceman's Lot* - Alan has recalled some interesting tales of that early post-war period. His abiding memory of the trade training course is clinging to the motor cycle pillion of a fellow airman as he was taken home on leave at break-neck speed. The book has moments of excitement, such as when he was employed on first-line servicing of Hawker Hunter aircraft. The greater part of his service was spent at RAF Duxford, a 'Battle of Britain' station near Cambridge.

Whilst researching this book, Alan paid a nostalgic visit to what is now part of the Imperial War Museum, known as IWM Duxford, the airfield he knew, with its vast collection of aircraft and regular air shows. Through the book I was able to revisit a way of life that I had found quite different from the normal. It had many exciting moments. This is the case with Alan's book. He began writing in 1990. His account of life in the RAF is his twelfth.   W R Mitchell

Introduction

The post war years were difficult ones for the RAF despite ending the Second World War with over one million personnel. Britain was virtually bankrupt at that time and could not afford to keep an Air Force of that size. Around seventy percent of its men and women were released and its aircraft were severely depleted as the supply of new ones virtually dried up. The old Lancaster and Lincoln bombers formed the backbone of Bomber Command as did many of the wartime fighter planes for Fighter Command. However, the current world situation demanded that a trained force was needed on stand-by in case of crises and the idea of conscripting young men for two years, training them and holding them in reserve, should they be required, was devised. It introduced thousands of them to service life and discipline, an activity they would surely have otherwise missed and I am sure that the majority of participants were strengthened by the experience and look back upon it as an unforgettable period of their lives.

Today, many people, especially the young, would look aghast if you were to suggest the return of National Service as a means of restoring discipline, but back in 2007, David Cameron, at that time leader of the opposition, proposed a modern-day return to National Service as being a possible answer to youth crime and disorder. He proposed a six-week National Citizen Service programme for problematic sixteen-year-olds, its aim being to test boys of that age and category whilst allowing their energy to contribute to society. It was not intended to be a complete return to National Service, but a mixture of community service and residential courses which culminated in a challenging mission. This sound idea was not taken up, but I think it would be a step in the right direction. Could it be expanded into a reduced form of National Service, say for a period of twelve months? Financial constraints aside, it would benefit many young people. My own experience was that you became more self-reliant and transformed from a boy into a man.

Fast forward to 2011 when the riots that broke out around the country prompted David Cameron to re-launch his notion of a National Citizen Service, which now sees thousands of volunteer sixteen-year-olds conduct summer projects to improve their communities.

David Cameron said: 'Many people have long thought that the answer to these questions of social behavior is to bring back National Service and in many ways I agree: Teamwork, discipline, duty, decency, these might sound old-fashioned words, but they are part of the solution to this very modern problem of alienated, angry young people.'

In my humble opinion these attributes are exactly the ones that National Service provided. It also fosters David Cameron's 'Big Society' as you look out for one another and form bonds that can last for a lifetime. Although National Service was a shock to the system for many conscripts and the first time they had left their homes and families, it was a time of great camaraderie. Young men, from varying backgrounds who had been thrown together in an alien situation, were made stronger by the discipline forced upon them and the knowledge that their new-found comrades would stand by them during a shared challenge.

It was these thoughts that prompted me to write this account of my experiences, which illustrate the life of a National Serviceman, dragged from his mother's apron strings, learning to take life by the scruff of the neck and enjoying the comradeship and broader horizons that military service provides.

I hope you enjoy this story, warts and all.

The author

CHAPTER ONE

Ministry of Labour and National Service demand my services. Induction at RAF Cardington

'Swing those arms or I'll tear 'em off and hit you with the soggy end!' These menacing words were part of my initiation into the RAF as a National Serviceman in June 1957. They were uttered by a Drill Instructor whilst our batch of raw recruits was undergoing 'square-bashing.' To be precise, we were being marched from the sick bay following a painful series of injections and being 'encouraged' to swing our sore arms as we marched.

To start at the beginning; a brown envelope dropped through the letterbox on the 19 April 1957. I opened it with some trepidation to find a letter inside headed 'National Service Acts.' The moment of truth had arrived. It was from the Ministry of Labour and National Service demanding my presence for a medical examination on the 27 April to ascertain if I was fit enough to serve 'Her Majesty.' The section concerning a travel warrant and overnight expenses, incurred in attending, had been crossed out. This was just as well, for I lived a mere fifteen minute's walk from the nearest Medical Board Centre. However, the allowances for loss of earnings and subsistence make interesting reading today. They were as follows:

Subsistence allowance (depending on distance from home to place attended) above 10 miles and under 20 miles, two shillings (10p), rising to six shillings (30P) for 60 miles and over. Where overnight absence is unavoidable an allowance of 15 shillings (75p) is made.

Compensation for loss of earnings is subject to a maximum of 30 shillings (£1.50)per day

I duly presented myself for an in-depth examination from top to toe, which included a hearing test where a man sat some distance away from me and whispered something that I foolishly whispered back. My knees were tapped with a rubber hammer to test my reflexes and I was told to cough whilst the doctor held a tender part, or should I say, two parts, of my

1

NATIONAL SERVICE ACTS

MINISTRY OF LABOUR AND NATIONAL SERVICE

Regional Office, R.O.6. (53),
Government Buildings (No. 2 Block),
Clifton Boulevard,

Registration No. *MDK. 34738.*   1 8 APR 57   NOTTINGHAM.
                                                          (Date)

> Mr. *A. PLOWRIGHT,*
> *52, ST. ANDREWS TERR.,*
> *MANSFIELD,*
> *NOTTS.*

DEAR SIR,

I have to inform you that in accordance with the National Service Acts you are required to submit yourself to medical examination by a medical board at *12-45* a.m. on *THURSDAY* day, *25 APR 57* 19........., at the Medical p.m.

Board Centre, ... Queens Hall, Belvedere Street, ... Mansfield, Notts. ....

If you wear glasses, you should bring them with you to the Medical Board.

On reporting for medical examination you should present this form and your Certificate of Registration (N.S.2 or N.S.62) to the clerk in charge of the waiting room.

* A Travelling Warrant for your return journey is enclosed. Before starting your journey you must exchange the warrant for a ticket at the booking office named on the warrant. You should take special care of the return half of the ticket as in the event of loss you will be required to obtain a fresh ticket at normal fare at your own expense.

* If you reside more than six miles from the Medical Board Centre and travel by omnibus or tram your fare will be paid at the Centre. (N.B. Reimbursement of fares is restricted to the cost of the cheapest means of travel.)

Any subsistence allowances which may become payable to you in accordance with the scale overleaf will be paid to you on application when you attend at the Medical Board Centre.

Immediately on receipt of this notice, you should inform your employer of the date and time at which you are required to attend for medical examination.

If you are called up you will receive a further notification giving you at least 14 days' notice, unless you have requested a shorter period of notice. You should accordingly not voluntarily give up your employment because you are required to attend for medical examination.

Your attention is directed to the Notes printed on the back of this Notice.

Yours faithfully,

N.S.6

* *Delete if not applicable.*   G. E. BROWN,   (P.T.O.)
   for Regional Controller

Notification of Medical Form

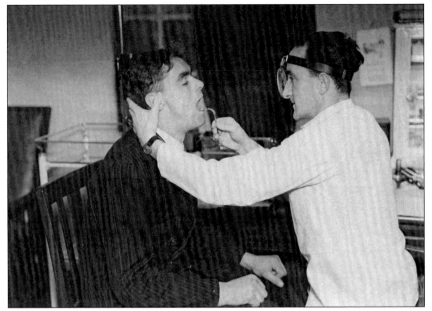

Open Wide!

anatomy. My eye test was a revelation. Despite having worn glasses for reading for some time I was assured that I did not need them. Remarkably, I passed the medical with flying colours. It was quite a shock to learn that I was A1 grade and as fit as a flea. Could it have been that if you were still warm and upright you had a good chance of passing?

After this news I was interviewed by an RAF officer to determine if I was fit to enter that service. Probably because of my having served a skilled apprenticeship and gained some qualifications I was told that I would be accepted.

The prison door had slammed behind me. I could almost hear the sound of heavy bolts sliding into place. No escaping two years without home comforts, particularly my own bed and teddy bear. My dreams of becoming an actor were put on hold, (Laurence Olivier heaved a huge sigh of relief) and numerous leisure activities were about to be curtailed.

The next communication, with a travel warrant included, from Her Majesty's armed forces demanded that I report to RAF Cardington in Bedfordshire. It arrived a mere week after my medical examination. They seemed eager to get me

You are in the RAF Now, Young Man!

in their clutches.

On the 27th May I took my first step into the wider world and reported to RAF Cardington. On my arrival I was intrigued to see two extremely large hangars, which, I discovered, were known as 'sheds' and were built to house airships. I also learned that Cardington became one of the major British sites responsible for the development of airships when the famous Short Brothers bought land here. The first 'shed' was built in 1915 to enable the construction of two rigid airships and by 1917 around 800 people were involved in the enterprise. The second 'shed' was dismantled at a naval establishment and rebuilt at Cardington in 1928. At that time the construction of the R101, an experimental rigid airship, was commenced as part of an Imperial Airship Scheme. This scheme was initiated to provide passenger and mail transport from Britain to the most distant parts of the British Empire. Unfortunately, the R101 crashed in France during its maiden overseas flight in 1930, killing forty-eight people. The loss of life was greater than the *Hindenburg* disaster of 1937 and the crash of the R101 effectively ended British use of rigid airships.

Kite Balloons in No.1 Shed, Cardington

Another feature that attracted my attention was the barrage balloons floating above the camp. In 1936 Cardington had begun their construction and became the No.1 RAF Balloon Training Unit. In fact, Cardington manufactured its own hydrogen in the 'Gas Factory,' as it was known, for the airships and balloons and by 1955 produced all the gasses used by the RAF until its closure in 2000.

Thus I was inducted into the loving arms of the RAF and fitted out with a uniform, comprising items such as shirts, 'three for the use of,' and 'soles plimp,' (trainers) for PT, according to the jovial storeman issuing them. He joked that if the various items of clothing fitted we must be deformed. Accessories, included a 'housewife,' no, not the human variety, but a much less exciting sewing kit for darning socks and sewing on buttons. An essential utensil was a pint mug for lashings of tea.

I was introduced to RAF food, which, in the main was passable. What it lacked in quality was counterbalanced by quantity, which was good for a person like me with a strong appetite. There was plenty of it – second helpings and you could fill any remaining gaps in the stomach with bread and jam. The only truly bad food was in Cyprus, where I was served with gristly meat balls floating in a sea of obnoxious gravy.

Like the phoney war of 1940 I spent the next seven days at Cardington in limbo, mooching around the camp and staring at the barrage balloons hovering above me whilst bemoaning my predicament. Desperate for some excitement I tried to imagine the scenario should one of those giant 'gasbags' burst.

At the end of this uneventful week things changed dramatically, almost making me yearn for the monotony of Cardington. One morning we were herded onto a train and transported to the pleasant Shropshire town of Bridgnorth. I say pleasant, what little we saw of it, for the only time I escaped the camp's clutches for the next eight weeks was when we were granted a few days mid-course leave. We were about to undergo what the RAF termed 'basic training,' but we came to know it as 'square-bashing.'

CHAPTER TWO

'Square-bashing' at RAF Bridgnorth

At the railway station we were met by fearsome NCO Drill Instructors (DI's), with eyes glinting beneath cap peaks lowered virtually to their foreheads and a menacing manner. Hustled into waiting lorries we were transported to the training camp on the outskirts of the town. Unused to such rough treatment we new recruits sat in gloomy silence until one of our number, who had been in the RAF before and re-enlisted, spoke. (Re-enlisted! I could not imagine any sane person signing on for more of this treatment.) He assured us that although things looked bleak at that moment they would improve. The downcast expressions of his companions signified that we did not believe a word of it.

When we arrived at the camp and prepared to alight from the lorries things became considerably worse. We were physically yanked from them whilst the DI's shouted, 'You have left the holiday camp now and you 'erks' (new recruits) will wish you had never been born!' We were thrust onto the parade ground and ordered to form up in rows. I stood quaking in my newly-issued boots listening to the mayhem and praying that I could die at that moment!

Eventually, when the lorries were unloaded we were marched to our various billets (huts). Each billet was assigned a flight (group of recruits) and several billets comprised a squadron. I became part of No.1 Flight, A Squadron. We were allocated a bed and a wardrobeand shown how to lay out our kit on our beds in a certain order. Blankets in a 'square pack' were placed at the head of the bed. This consisted of three neatly folded blankets wrapped around with a further one, giving a square shape. As a refinement, pieces of cardboard could be placed between the sides of the folded blankets and the outer one to produce a more regular shape. Clothes, 'eating irons' (knife fork and spoon), boot/shoe cleaning kit, 'Brasso' (for buttons, buckles and badges), and 'housewife' all had their place. Pint mugs were prominent and required to be spotlessly clean. At the end of this instruction we were informed there would be a kit inspection in one hour.

Two DI's duly arrived for the inspection and tore through the hut like a plague of locusts. Square packs were torn open. Blankets, clothes and various items lay in heaps in their wake. Mugs were thrown at the two coal-burning stoves in the middle of the hut, smashing them to pieces (the mugs, not the stoves!) Their actions were accompanied by maniacal shouts. 'Disgusting!' 'pathetic!' 'a disgrace to the RAF!' were some of the terms of endearment thrown at us. The cowering recruits recoiled when their turn came, petrified by this 'tour de force'and some were almost in tears. 'It's no good crying for your mummy,' they were told, 'I'm your mummy now and you had better get used to it!'

We were warned that if there was no improvement on further inspections we would be put on a charge. To avoid this punishment during morning kit inspections, one or two recruits laid out their kit on the previous evening and slept on the floor. If put on a charge it meant reporting to your DI after the day's activities and performing some demeaning task such as cleaning, washing the latrines, or polishing the DI's boots and brasses (buttons, badges and belt buckles). As we discovered, this was nothing compared to the threat of being 'back-flighted,' which meant being made to serve an extra week's training in that hell-hole. This punishment was held over our heads for six out of the eight-week training course, until one day our DI's bluff was called. Our flight was lined up outside our hut undergoing rifle drill and he was tearing into us, as was normal, for our 'sloppy display,' as he called it. We were threatened with drilling from morning till night until we improved. 'If any of you ingrates can't stand this,' we were informed, 'you can be back-flighted.' 'How many of you want that?' we were asked. At that moment a large vehicle approached along the strip of concrete on which we were stood in formation. It was too large to get past all of us and half of the squad stepped forward to allow it access, as though in answer to the DI's threat. He was lost for words. The brow-beaten recruits began to laugh and even the DI struggled to avoid a smile, before recovering his composure and treating us to more invective.

Another part of our initiation into RAF life was the

obligatory haircut, or should I say, scalp. It was more akin to sheep-shearing. The camp barbers' shears worked overtime removing treasured luxurious locks, which landed in piles on the floor, and we were rendered almost bald. At least there was no chance of hair falling into your eyes whilst drilling. Our photographs were taken for identification purposes. We resembled criminals on wanted posters with our shorn locks and miserable expressions.

By that stage of our training we had, thankfully, a more human DI than our initial one, a short, Scottish beast of a man whose aim appeared to make all recruit's lives a living hell. He continually shouted abuse as we marched and drilled, nearly leaving the floor as he spat out his invective. I reckoned that some DI's are born mean and vindictive. The parade ground was the perfect place for these bullies who lack any shred of decency or humanity. Thank goodness this Scottish ogre had only three more days to serve in the RAF when our batch of recruits arrived. We were not aware of this at the time and we were mightily relieved when he disappeared, never to return.

Another lesson learned was to always concentrate on your tasks and drill, thereby never allowing the DI's to find out your name. If they did you would never be left alone, which only made things worse as you were humiliated before your fellow recruits and if you were of a sensitive nature your entire spirit could be broken. We had one such unfortunate airman in our flight that was reduced to a quivering wreck.

After the initial battering, life became a little more worth living and humour began to surface as we became used to the constant badgering and abuse. We realized that the DI's were not allowed to swear at recruits and marvelled at their ingenuity in finding words to demean us such as 'thick wretch,' 'mummy's pride and joy' and 'first-class cretin.' Recruits who were exceptionally tall and gangling were pounced upon; 'I didn't know they piled manure that high!' Fortunately, not being able to swear at us took the sting out of their abuse. If these tall unfortunates could not march smartly, they were scolded by the DI with, 'Oi! You marching like a pregnant fairy, smarten yourself laddie!' A classic example of their repertoire was performed after we had attended the medical

RAF Bridgnorth – Main Gate

room for injections, as I mentioned at the outset. As we left and marched away we were ordered to swing our punctured and painful arms as high as we could, accompanied by, 'You 'orrible scum, swing those arms or I'll tear 'em off and hit you with the soggy end!'

Another incident served to raise our spirits and it concerned our supposedly dirty mugs being smashed on the stoves. One member of our flight, who had been put on a charge, had to clean the brasses of our DI, which gave him access to the instructor's room. Whilst in there he noticed a broom with its handle ringed by many mug handles and we discovered that the DI's held competitions to see how many mugs they could smash and kept the severed handles on a broom handle to check on their accomplishments.

For a little light relief we gave each other nicknames, with such gems as: 'Crusoe' (Robinson), 'Feathers' (Peacock), 'Jabbie' (Wainwright - scared of injections), 'Snoggy' (Tucker – fancied himself as a 'Romeo') and 'Wat' (Harry Tyler, who incidentally, came from my home town). After 'lights out' we swopped tales and jokes (some outrageous), which helped

RAF Bridgnorth – No.1 Flight, 'A' Squadron

to relax us before falling asleep. Amongst them, our favourites concerned what we would like to do to the DI's. Here is a selection of the more printable ones with an RAF theme:

'What's the difference between a fighter pilot and a jet engine? Answer, a jet engine stops whining when the plane shuts down.' (Uttered by the airman who had re-enlisted).

'Right you cretins, snarled the swine of a DI, I suppose when you're released from the RAF you'll be waiting for me to die so you can pee (milder word) on my grave.'

'A Flight Lieutenant was driving down a muddy back road in his RAF Landrover when he met another vehicle of the same type stuck in the mud with an angry Squadron Leader sat in it. 'Is your Landrover stuck, sir?' asked the Flight Lieutenant. 'No,' replied the Squadron Leader, handing him the keys, 'Yours is!'

Two examples of famous last words:
'Of course it's a dummy round.'
'Sweep it under the bed, the DI will never notice.'

A recruit swore that prior to a passing out parade his flight was given the procedure for fainting by a DI. It went as follows:

'If you feel faint whilst on parade you will fall at attention in a smart, orderly fashion and not slump in an untidy heap!'

As the weeks passed we were put through a strict timetable of drill, both marching and rifle. In fact we were constantly marching. In addition to the marching drill outside our billet we were marched to the canteen, parade ground and outdoor training area, also around the camp. As usual our ears were invaded by the dulcet tones of the DI. 'Dig those heels in!' was a familiar cry. We were ordered to do this to produce the sound of multiple metal-tipped boot heels hitting tarmac simultaneously. That was the intention, but the result was not always straight-forward. There was usually some poor recruit out of step. Another variation was the 'tick-tock' man, as the DI's dubbed them. These were recruits who could not swing their arms in unison with their fellow-recruits. This was because their right arm automatically moved forward at the same time as the right leg, which caused the DI's tremendous consternation. The poor unfortunates blessed with this handicap were mercilessly persecuted. Despite this some found it impossible to break the habit and were banned from the 'passing-out' parade at the end of our training.

The DI's requirement that every exercise was performed in unison applied also to rifle and bayonet drill. At the command 'fix bayonets' they were required to be fitted to the barrel of the rifle and snapped into place with an audible click. As usual we were expected to perform this task as one, resulting in a loud 'click.' Usually, the opposite happened and there was a series of clicks, which sent the DI into another tirade.

For periods of weapon and Brengun (a light–weight, quick-firing machine gun) training and ground combat activities we marched to the outdoor training area dressed in poorly-fitting and shapeless denim overalls. I actually excelled during one lesson of mock warfare when we were required to crawl across a supposed battlefield (scrub land) on our bellies, gripping our rifles like grim death whilst the instructor ran alongside hurling abuse and timing us. I completed the course in the fastest time and was even offered a cigarette, which was not much of a reward, for I am a non smoker.

The task of stripping and re-assembling the rifle and Bren

gun was a stressful affair as it was performed under the beady eye of an instructor, often shouting, 'Come on, come on, get a move on, if it had hair round it you'd find its slot in no time!'

Training with the bayonet, as used in warfare, was a hoot. Our targets were dummies dangling on ropes and, one at a time we were made to charge at these effigies with fixed bayonets, whilst screaming and hollering, then plunging our bayonets into the supposed enemy. Once again it did not turn out quite like the instructions. All the recruits could muster was a few pathetic whines that petered out as they stumbled towards the dummies, most of whom were unharmed when stabbed with our bayonets as they merely moved aside. Fortunately, one of our band got into the spirit of the task and galloped towards his target with a blood-curdling yell - 'Dacey (the name of our DI) you b ...a...s...t...a...r...d!' before skewering the poor dummy with a violent thrust. The honour of the flight had been preserved.

The firing range was not without incident. We were instructed to fire at small targets about thirty yards away and given a lecture, sorry, a rant, about safety when using live ammunition. 'If any of you numbskulls shoot me,' threatened the instructor, 'I'll come back and haunt you and give you the 'screaming abdabs.' Despite the warnings one member of our flight found that his rifle had jammed. The fool stood up still holding out his rifle and turned towards the instructor, who leapt about a foot into the air and screamed, 'Point the sodding thing at the target, you useless retard!' Unfortunately, few of our number rose to the dizzy heights of 'marksman,' some missed the target altogether. I did quite well, but narrowly failed to attain a marksman's badge.

The 'piece de resistance' was the assault course, a daunting series of obstacles to be surmounted. There were extremely high fences to be scaled, nets to crawl under, logs to be run along and muddy ditches to be crossed by means of ropes. All these activities were accompanied by the obligatory verbal abuse from the instructors. An abiding memory of these antics was the sight of a recruit wearing 'bottle-bottom' glasses leap for a rope in order to swing across one of the ditches, completely miss it and fall face down in the mud. The poor man said, scraping the mud from his eyes, 'I could see two ropes and

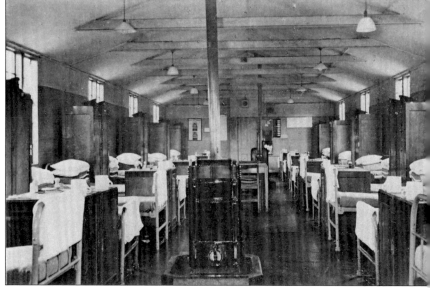

RAF Bridgnorth – Interior of a Hut

jumped for the wrong one!'

One blessed short release from the mayhem of this outdoor training was the arrival of the 'chuck-wagon' bearing char (tea) and wads (donuts). Ravenous recruits, appetites honed by manic physical activity, descended on the vehicle and stripped it bare of its cargo.

During all this activity we had other exciting events, such as F.F.I. inspections to check your cleanliness and freedom from certain diseases. We were lined up in the medical centre and made to strip off every item of clothing. The medics inspected each one of us, which included a close examination of our private parts. An essential piece of the doctor's equipment was a pencil that they used to lift your member to allow ultra close examination. It made me feel glad that I would never have a job like theirs.

As if we were not exhausted enough with all the drilling, 'bulling' and outdoor activities, we endured periods of physical training in the gymnasium. Here we were subjected to various forms of physical torture by bullying PT instructors, which included leaping over vaulting-horses, hanging from wall bars,

RAF Bridgnorth – Occupants of Hut 22. The author is seated on the ground to the left of the shield

lifting unyielding weights or contorting our bodies into unnatural shapes. No sinew was left unstretched and there was no joint that did not ache.

In the midst of all this activity the RAF deemed that sex was off the menu, which was a laugh because we were far too exhausted. Rumours were rife that the canteen and NAAFI staff laced our tea and coffee with bromide to dampen our libido, which was totally unnecessary, for we never got the chance to mix with the opposite sex.

The mention of sex recalls the memory of one recruit, who, longing for relief from our chaste existence, wrote to a national newspaper requesting the inclusion of his pleading missive in its 'Letters' column. It contained a heart-rending tale of privation and longing for female contact during his harsh treatment at the hands of the RAF and he wrote that if any young ladies would care to correspond with him it would transform his humdrum existence. Little did he realise the impact this would have on a sympathetic female public for he was inundated with replies from all parts of the country. There were not exactly sack-loads of mail, but he received so many letters it came to the notice of the DI's who christened him 'Romeo,' a name that they delighted in shouting out when the daily supply of mail was issued to the flight whilst assembled on parade. I do not know if he formed a lasting relationship with any of his correspondents, but it took him a good part of each evening to read his mail. Of course, several other recruits taunted him and offered to take some of the ladies off of his hands.

On the other side of the coin, another airman received a 'Dear John' letter from his girlfriend who had presumably grown tired of his absence and found a more accessible boyfriend. The letter did not go down very well with its jilted recipient who transferred the offending ex-girlfriend's photograph from his bedside locker to the dartboard in the NAFFI and used it for target practice!

These two events added a little brightness to our ordeal, which was sorely needed during the evenings, for I have ingrained memories of many 'bull nights' spent sprucing up the billet, which had to be maintained in immaculate condition. This included polishing the floor until you could almost see your reflection in it and all the fittings including the stoves and pulling a lightly-oiled rag ('four by two') through the barrel of my rifle in order to keep it spotlessly clean and thus avoid the wrath of our DI. Toecaps of our boots were made to shine like mirrors with the application of spit and polish, the latter applied in large quantities and spread with a heated spoon in a circular motion. Oceans of 'Brasso' was used for the polishing of buttons, buckles and badges. Trousers had to be pressed with a crease you could almost cut your finger on and this was normally achieved with damp brown paper and a very hot iron (not hot enough to set fire to the paper!). Some recruits tried to circumvent this task by placing their trousers between the mattress and bedstead, which was not encouraged. An airman who was caught using this practice was put on a charge for being 'idle whilst asleep!'

During these chores there was the consolation of hearing the latest pop songs on the hut radio. When I close my eyes today I can still hear the 'laid-back' Perry Como's dulcet tones crooning *A White Sports Coat and a Pink Carnation*, or Pat

Boone gliding through *I'll be Home* in his gentle, soothing style.

Sometimes a recruit would suffer bullying, but this was often because he was not pulling his weight with shared duties or did not put his back into tasks and got the flight into trouble. However, the opposite could apply in exchanges of skills for such chores as sewing on buttons, ironing or cleaning brasses. One member of our flight reckoned that these tasks should only be done by women and would not demean himself by doing them. He got round this by paying some of his companions to do them for him. This worked well in his case, but he was in the favourable position of coming from a moneyed family and did not have to rely on the pittance paid by the RAF. For the rest of us it was a case of rallying round and helping a recruit who was helpless at some of the tasks, even to the extent of writing letters for those who found it difficult.

Another diversion was guard duty, though why anyone in his right mind would wish to gain unauthorised access to the camp was beyond me. They would be seriously outnumbered by those trying to get out. On one occasion I was on duty at the main gate and had been instructed not to let anyone enter without a pass. During my stint an open-top sports car driven by a dashing Flight Lieutenant screeched to a halt outside the gate. 'Let me in old chap,' he said, his scarf fluttering in the breeze. I saluted and replied, 'Could I see your pass, please sir?' 'Haven't got it with me,' he replied. 'Sorry sir,' I said, 'but you can't come in without a pass.' The officer's hackles began to rise. 'Don't be silly man, I am based here,' he said. Apologetically, I insisted that he could not enter. His neck above the scarf began to redden. 'You silly fellow!' he yelled, 'I tell you I'm from the camp!' He placed his hand on the horn and left it there. The noise brought the duty sergeant dashing from the nearby guardroom. When he saw who was in the car, he saluted and asked, 'Is there a problem, sir?' He obviously knew the irate officer. 'Of course there's a ruddy problem, this airman says I can't enter.' The sergeant became very apologetic. 'I'm awfully sorry, sir,' he replied, 'you go right ahead.' As the Flight Lieutenant drove through the gates the sergeant glared at me before returning to the guardroom. So much for not letting

RAF Bridgnorth – Passing Out Parade

anyone into the camp without a pass, I thought.

One day there was a flap on over an imminent visit and inspection of the camp by the Group AOC (Air Officer Commanding). The DI's created an even stronger air of apprehension as frantic preparations got underway. Anything that did not move was painted and the zenith of our sprucing up of the camp was cutting the grass around our billet with scissors! Mercifully, we escaped unscathed as the inspection passed off without any disasters and there was no 'back-flighting.'

With the passage of time our hair had begun to grow and its inspection formed part of morning parade where our uniform and appearance was scrutinised. A favourite expression of the DI as he walked behind you was, 'Am I hurting you laddie? . . .' Cos I'm standing on your bleedin' hair!' If it remained the same length at the next morning's inspection you were put on a charge.

We were let out of camp for an exercise known as 'R and I,' (Reliability and Initiative), where we would live under canvas and, supposedly, perform various tasks such as survival and

Bridgnorth – Remembrance Day Parade in the High Street

backwoodsman skills. What a farce it turned out to be. We piled into trucks and were taken on a substantial journey before being deposited in a clearing within the confines of a large and dense forest. No means of escape for the faint-hearted beckoned and no sooner had we pitched our tents than it began to rain. It rained . . . and rained . . . and rained, turning the camp into a quagmire. Without any show of reliability or initiative our instructors told us to dismantle our tents and prepare to leave. It was with mixed feelings that I carried out this order. One part of me was relieved at not having to demonstrate my survival skills, yet on the other we were supposed to be battle-hardened by now. How could we return to Bridgnorth with our tails between our legs and admit that we were frightened by a drop of rain? I have been forced to live with the memory of this infamy for over fifty years!

After several weeks of exercise, fresh air and substantial amounts of food we began to put on weight as we developed muscle to replace flab. On returning home for the mid-course leave my parents mentioned how fit I looked but seemed more reserved. My reticence was due no doubt to the thought of returning to camp for a further session of character-building. Four more weeks only, I kept reminding myself. One consolation was to wear my uniform during the leave. How impressive I looked, I imagined, until I passed a couple of men in the street, one of who declared, 'Look at that bloody hat!' He was referring to my pristine cap whose top was flat as a pancake rather than the more individualistic shapes that seasoned airmen moulded them into.

During the latter stages of our training course we were regularly threatened with failing to make the grade for the fast-approaching 'passing-out' parade, which would delay our escape from torment. The DI's went to town on us - drilling and more drilling till we ached, our feet had blisters on our blisters and the 'bull' sessions became more intense. Brasses were polished till they shone, boots were even deeper cleaned and toecaps gleamed. Uniforms were pressed, billet floors polished even more vigorously with 'bumpers' (a heavy mop) and the cast iron stoves were black-leaded with extra care.

It was lucky that my training took place in July and August, for we heard tales of the harsh condition of the billets in winter. The stoves, apparently, glowed red at night - that is, when you could get coal and the billet would be invaded by noxious fumes. Health and Safety inspectors would have had a field day in those days, only if they had awakened from induced carbon monoxide poisoning!

An important examination took place during the last stage of our training when we were required to go before a trade-selection team. If you had signed on as a 'regular' you were more or less guaranteed your requested trade for the duration of your service. National Servicemen had to undergo an in-depth test by the team to assess their suitability for various occupations, taking account of qualifications and experience. Luckily, I was given the post of airframe mechanic, which was not too far removed from my job in civilian life. I had served a five-year engineering apprenticeship as a press toolmaker, (having been 'deferred' until the age of twenty-one). Many unfortunate National Servicemen were given unenviable positions bearing no relationship to the ones they preferred. A recruit with whom I had become friends had six GCEs and applied for pilot training. He failed his eyesight test and was given the post of nursing attendant second class, a complete waste of two years to be spent in the medical centre, probably keeping records and acting as a stretcher-bearer.

With the end of the course fast approaching our drill sessions became even more onerous and our thoughts became filled by the demanding 'passing-out' parade, where all the recruits would perform on the parade square before a crowd of dignitaries, relatives and friends. As previously mentioned, 'tick-tock' men were banned from taking part in the display and it was woe betide any recruit that made a hash of the drill. The honour of our flight, in fact, the whole contingent, we were told was at stake by our erstwhile DI's. The cynical amongst us reckoned they were scared of getting it in the neck if we did not come up to scratch.

Finally the great day arrived and we marched to the square, 'battle-hardened' and spruced up to the nines, determined to show what training and hard work we had undergone. The parade went off very smoothly and we even felt proud as we drilled in unison before parents, wives and girl-friends.

What a relief it was to leave Bridgnorth behind and travel home for a well-earned leave before reporting to our various trade-training camps, carrying a load of memories, which, despite the hardships we had experienced would remain with us for the rest of our lives.

In later life, out of nostalgia, I sought more information concerning the camp and discovered that it opened in 1939 and closed in 1963.

It began life at Stanmore, close to Bridgnorth, but could not be given that name as RAF Stanmore already existed, in Middlesex. Each year many visitors who served and were trained at the camp re-visit the site of their introduction to the RAF. Today little remains of the base and its former site now resides in Stanmore Country Park, cared for by Bridgnorth parks department, an area of tranquility set amid Stanmore Industrial Estate. It also houses a War Memorial in the form of a chimney embellished with a plaque. There are benches in a circle for use by older veterans and visitors. The memorial plaque was attached to the chimney in 1944 and a fly-past, which included a Supermarine Spitfire, was held during the ceremony.

The training camp began life in November 1939, not long after the beginning of World War II and, although not fully operational until several months later, it was eventually occupied by around 3000 recruits and 500 instructors. The recruits usually arrived at the town by train and residents recall them marching through Low Town and up the hill to the base.

During 1940 it was also used as a transit camp and kit-issuing centre for large numbers of Czech, Polish, French, Belgian and Dutch forces evacuated from the Continent at the fall of France.

In 1941 the station received a visit from HRH the Princess Royal and shortly after this grand occasion the recruits were transferred and the new occupier was the Women's Auxiliary Air Force (WAAF). In 1942 the roles were reversed and WAAF training ceased and the RAF returned, to carry on recruit training. The new routine involved ground combat and navigation instruction, and in 1944 it was extended to include air gunners and wireless operators.

It has been said that Adolf Hitler intended to use Bridgnorth as his flying base after his victory over England in the Second World War! In 1942, because the station did not possess any runways, the RAF brought damaged aircraft, ranging from Spitfires to Lancasters and positioned them around the camp to give the impression of an active airfield. After the war some of the aircraft were rebuilt or put on display in RAF museums.

During October 1945 air training ceased and ground service training was resumed. In March of that year King George VI approved a crest for the station that contained the caption, 'This is the gate, the walls are men.' The emblem is a torch and portcullis.

German prisoners of war were held at the station from 1946 to 1947 and at Christmas 1946 they provided a party for the children of the RAF staff. Two years later 3,000 people attended the first of several Tattoos there with 1,000 airmen participating. The event included a fly-past by a de Havilland Vampire and a formation flight of Lancaster bombers.

In April 1950 the base became the first in the RAF to be awarded The Freedom of Entry to the Borough, a status that allowed RAF personnel to enter and march in the town with full colours.

I have discovered some famous names that are associated with RAF Bridgnorth. Cyril Washbrook the Lancashire and England cricketer was a Physical Training Instructor during the Second World War (1941- 1942). He was married whilst serving there. Des O'Connor, the entertainer, trained at RAF Bridgnorth in 1949, as did Ronnie Corbett. Ramon Subba Row the Northants and England opener was a Flight Commander from 1956 to 1958.

Today there is an organisation known as Bridgnorth Veterans and reunion parades by their number have taken place in recent years. The one that was held in 2009 had added interest for the participants, which arose with the re-discovery of the RAF Bridgnorth Drill Cup. This is a trophy that was presented to the flight that excelled at drill during their training and was much coveted. Unfortunately, my particular flight did not receive the honour, but I was content with performing without disaster at the 'passing-out' parade!

The cup was retrieved by Peter Williams a member of the winning flight of his intake after much ferreting detective work. When the station closed in 1963 the Stanmore site was auctioned by a local firm that Peter approached at the outset of his quest in 2006. They were unable to help but Peter gathered through contact with various websites that the cup had been moved to RAF Swinderby, the station that had taken over from Bridgnorth for basic training. This proved of little help as Swinderby had closed some years ago, and the trail went cold. It was a chance visit to the RAF Museum at Hendon in 2009 that led to contact with the MOD (Ministry of Defence) and he received a prompt reply to his request for information concerning the cup, which turned out to be good news. The cup had been found and was kept at RAF Halton. Peter was given a sympathetic response to his request for the trophy to be released in time for the Bridgnorth reunion and his search had finally been successful after two and a half years.

In July 2010 the unveiling of a Memorial Stone was celebrated in the town. Following months of preparation, representatives from Bridgnorth Town Council, RAF Cosford and veterans of RAF Bridgnorth gathered at Lavington Hole Gardens, not far from the terminus of the cable railway in Low Town. The ceremony was to commemorate the links forged between civic and military organisations and between the townspeople and recruits during1939-1963.

In her remarks the Lady Mayor referred proudly to the bonds that were forged between the people of the town and the recruits. She also mentioned that during the unveiling they were beside the route that had been taken by each new intake of recruits from the railway station that would be unaware they were passing a site where a simple ceremony would one day commemorate their time at the camp.

The plaque itself bears the following inscription:

This memorial commemorates the bond that exists between the people of Bridgnorth and the former Air Force Station Bridgnorth (1939-1963). It records the contribution to world peace during those years of conflict by the men and women who were trained there.

CHAPTER THREE

Trade Training at RAF Kirkham

Following my appearance in the 'passing-out' parade at RAF Bridgnorth I had a joyous journey home and a period of leave before reporting to the Trade Training camp, RAF Kirkham, situated between Preston and Blackpool. I would report there as AC2 (Aircraftsman Second Class) Plowright, (service number 5045445, which I have never forgotten), the lowest of the low in rank and paid the most princely sum of two pounds twelve shillings and sixpence per week. However, hopes were high that it would be a more 'cushy' life than that at Bridgnorth and I would be based a reasonable distance from my home in Mansfield.

I journeyed via Manchester to the RAF station in September of 1957 with the knowledge that I would undergo three months of training as an airframe mechanic, ('rigger' in RAF parlance). My billet was similar to that at Bridgnorth. No doubt the RAF had a similar design throughout much of the service. The camp was officially known as the No. 10 School of Technical Training for Airframes and Armament. It had opened in 1940 and in the following year became the main armament training centre for the RAF with pupils from many countries attending its courses. After World War II it became a demob (demobilisation) centre.

Thankfully, at my new station, restrictions were relaxed in respect of free time. At nights and weekends we were allowed off camp and I managed to get home most weekends, courtesy of a fellow trainee named Melvin who I was lucky to befriend and who lived not far from my home. He had a motorcycle and I spent many a hair-raising hour clinging to the pillion as it traversed the steep hills and winding roads of Lancashire, Cheshire and Derbyshire at breakneck speed. On the few occasions when my fellow trainee was unavailable I made the journey to and from home by train, which was a lengthy and laborious process.

The airframe course that I undertook was very thorough and enlightening. In fact it turned out to be almost too thorough, for much of the information was not used, but it was all of interest to me having an engineering background. When I got to my first squadron I was asking all kinds of technical questions and received blank stares or the reply, 'You don't need all that stuff.'

For those of you with an interest in aircraft the elements of the course covered a comprehensive range of systems and operations. We learnt about the fabric of the airframe and its repair, also the flight control systems, including ailerons, elevators, rudders, flaps and trim tabs. I realise that such technicalities may be yawn-inducing, for which I apologise, but for the avid engineers I will add integrated air systems (pneumatics, air conditioning and temperature control) basic electrical systems, landing gear and undercarriage construction and finally hydraulic power systems. It was similar to going back to school, but it had the added benefit of preparing young men for a trade in 'civvy street' when their service was completed. All the imparted information, together with diagrams, was entered in exercise books, for use when we were assigned to our various stations. These books would also be beneficial to those servicemen who would pursue a career in civil aviation on their return to civilian life.

In addition to our studies it was ensured that we kept fit by regular periods of PT and sport. I had played club rugby union since leaving school and volunteered for rugby training in the evenings, which resulted in a shock on my first training session for that sport. The PT activities during daytime consisted of 'circuit training,' during which we completed a series of exercises in rotation. Initially we were set a target under the watchful eye of an instructor by performing as many of each exercise as we could manage. Based on this we were given a reasonable number to complete for the forthcoming periods. The initial trial was very exhausting, so it was helpful that we were not compelled to reach those levels on a regular basis. The shock occurred when I reported for rugby training on the evening following my trial. I was asked by the coach to go round the circuit and do as many of each exercise as I could! When I explained that I was still exhausted from my efforts earlier that day I was told, 'Well just do what you can,' which

Technical Training on the hydraulic systems of aircraft

turned out to be one, or occasionally two of each exercise.

I thought I had left square-bashing behind, but our flight was chosen to perform marching and rifle drill in nearby Preston as part of the Remembrance Day celebrations that coming November. Many hours were spent drilling until we became quite proficient and were considered good enough to perform our routine outside the Guild Hall after parading through the centre of Preston. I was quite apprehensive about appearing in public, but on that cold November morning our exhibition passed off successfully and we received considerable applause for our efforts.

Some evenings were spent in the colourful and exciting resort of Blackpool, as my time at Kirkham coincided with its famous 'Lights' season. Thousands flocked to see the impressive illuminations, best viewed from the trams that conveyed sightseers to and fro along its six-mile promenade. The streets and amusement arcades were heaving with holidaymakers and visitors and the pleasure beach drew children (both young and grown up!) like a magnet. It was heady stuff to a National Serviceman after the privation of square-bashing. Theatres, the famous Tower Ballroom and the Winter Gardens were bursting at the seams. What an experience it was to ascend the Tower and enjoy the magnificent array of lights beneath that transformed the evening sky into a sea of colour.

I watched people pouring into the town's premier theatre, the Grand, which is still going strong and features currently amongst the top eight percent of listed building in England. I have always had a great interest in the theatre, having belonged to an amateur dramatic society up to the age of twenty-one, when this activity was curtailed, unfortunately, by the RAF. I did resume after National Service for several years, but work commitments intervened. The Grand is a beautiful and opulent theatre, completed in 1894, for the princely sum of £20,000, which is equivalent to £80,000,000 at today's value. It boasts some fine post-Baroque neoclassical architecture and as I surveyed the crowds entering its welcoming portals I could see clearly their anticipation as they sensed that they were entering another world.

The theatre was owned initially by Thomas Sergenson and designed by Frank Matcham, a renowned architect responsible for creating several splendid theatres, such as the London Coliseum. The opening performance was of very high quality, it was Shakespeare's *Hamlet* and in the first few weeks it presented the biggest musical hit of that period, *Charlie's Aunt*. In 1909 Sergenson sold the theatre to the Blackpool Tower Company for £47,500 and they ran it for the following 63 years.

Thankfully the theatre has survived the thorny path experienced by all such places of entertainment over the years. It is now in the hands of the Blackpool Grand Theatre Trust Limited, which reopened the establishment in 1981, following sterling work by the 'Friends of the Grand,' a society that was formed in 1973 to prevent its demolition. In addition to financial donations from its members over £750,000 was raised towards its refurbishment. Restoration work has taken place, aided recently by grants from the Arts Council, National Lottery and English Heritage and some of the 'Friends' assisted with decoration and repairs. Their good work has contributed towards the Grand becoming known as the 'National Theatre of Variety' in 2006.

A trainee Radio Fitter (the author's double!) checks the wireless equipment in a Vampire fighter-bomber

Listed among the 'Friends of the Grand,' are many famous performers, such as Ken Dodd and Violet Carson, two Lancastrians. Ken Dodd is probably better known to the younger generation as he is still performing at the age of eighty-five. Sadly, Violet died in 1983, but is renowned for her role as Ena Sharples in *Coronation Street,* now commonly known as 'Corrie.' Over her many appearances as Ena she built a reputation as a stoney-faced and blunt harridan, but she was far from that character in real life. She was an accomplished pianist and a regular member of *Children's Hour,* on the BBC Home Service, as it was in those days. As a child she performed with her sister around the theatres as a singing act called The Carson Sisters and then played piano accompaniment to silent films. Her prowess as a pianist led to her becoming a regular on Wilfred Pickles' popular radio show *Have a Go* in the 1940's/1950's. Violet never forgot her Lancashire roots and died aged eighty-five at her home in Blackpool.

Ken Dodd was born in Notty Ash, a district of Liverpool. He is known for his unruly mop of hair, prominent front teeth and the feather duster (tickling stick) that he uses in his act. His trademark line, 'Have you ever been tickled, missus?' is accompanied by the brandishing of the said duster. He has been a firm favourite with children over many years through his 'Diddymen' and was a fine singer in his prime, selling more than 1,000,000 records throughout the world. An entertainer in the style of the music hall comedian, he is still drawing the crowds today and has been known to entertain theatre audiences with marathon performances until the early hours of the morning. He holds the record for the greatest number of jokes related in one performance - 1500 in three and a half hours! A little known fact is that Ken has also made appearances as a straight actor that include performing in Shakespearean productions such as *Twelfth Night* and *Hamlet.*

These two fine performers, together with a host of others have made the Grand Theatre, with its fine tradition, what it is today, a place to entertain and perhaps bring a little light relief to audiences in these troubled times of recession and cut-backs.

During my spell at RAF Kirkham we were required to do night guard duty, which was rather unwelcome because the night roster was two hours on and two off, which meant little sleep. The former involved cycling around the camp, a boring pastime, during which the main objective was keeping awake, for we never saw anyone around apart from those in the guardhouse. During the two hours off it was very hard to get any sleep and just as you were finally dropping off an NCO would wake you up for your next spell. What we were supposed to be guarding was a mystery and, as at Bridgnorth, we wondered why anyone would wish to break into the camp. I did not imagine it was to steal the only aircraft on the station, a battered old Gloster Meteor that was used for demonstration purposes and was not airworthy. Members of our flight even had their photographs taken alongside this aircraft, with its damaged tailplane clearly in view. I am probably doing an injustice to the Meteor, which was the first jet plane to go into service with the RAF. It reigned supreme from 1949 to 1954 when thirty front line fighter squadrons were equipped with them. At that time it was the RAF's principal single-seat day fighter aircraft and it was rather sad to see the state of our neglected example.

That autumn a virulent strain of flu (referred to as 'Asian' by everyone) permeated the camp, claiming many victims. The main objective at that time was not missing out on leave and many who contracted the virus would struggle on until the weekend. Unfortunately, several never succeeded and we were sometimes awakened in the middle of the night by bodies falling on the floor and being carted off to the sick bay. I was very lucky because my symptoms appeared whilst I was on leave and I was able to stay at home for a week to recover. Even after that interval the virus was not completely thrown off, and during its most telling phase you felt like death.

Eventually, the end of the course loomed and our heads were full of so much knowledge I reckoned we knew everything about airframes and systems, but I was to be proved wrong when posted to a station. The culmination of the course was an oral examination, which, if failed, meant being back-flighted (horror of horrors!) and re-sitting it. Luckily, my examiner was very laid back and asked a few casual questions before announcing that I had passed.

RAF Kirkham - The occupants of Hut 29. The author is on the front row second from the right. Note the damaged Meteor!

On our last day the postings were read out before the assembled trainees. Mine was to RAF Tangmere, of which I knew nothing. As the name was read out the trainee next to me gave a gasp. 'That's in North Africa!' he said. He thought the officer had said Tangier! I was comforted by the thought that this was probably an educational posting, for which I had applied upon my entrance to the RAF. I should mention that in addition to my airframe course I had been carrying on with my mechanical engineering studies that I had somewhat neglected during my apprenticeship due to my numerous other interests. Consequently, I had fallen two years behind and by the age of twenty-one had only obtained an Ordinary National Certificate in Mechanical Engineering and still had two further years to study for the Higher National Certificate, which was my aim. The RAF very kindly allowed me to study at various technical colleges during my service and at that time I was attending a college in Preston three nights per week. This meant that in addition to my RAF studies I had homework to do on free nights and at weekends. An educational posting to RAF

*Rehearsing for the Remembrance Day drill display in Preston.
The author is on the front row second from the left*

Tangmere gave me the opportunity to carry on my studies.In my first year of service I attended three colleges and even sat the penultimate level exam at a base in Scotland, on my own with an officer invigilating, more about that later. Despite this hard work I fared better than one poor trainee who hailed from St. Andrews and applied for an overseas posting. He ended up at RAF Leuchars, a few miles from his home!

What of RAF Kirkham remains today? Sadly, nothing, for it is a category D prison. (This would have been apt for RAF Bridgnorth!) It was taken over by the Home Office in the early 1960's. The infrastructure and services, together with most of the buildings are of World War Two vintage, though prisoner accommodation is relatively new. All prisoners are those who can be reasonably trusted to serve their sentence in open conditions. All rooms have Freeview TV and three dormitories have en-suite facilities, including showers. Prisoners also have access to in-room TV. (Conditions are considerably better than when Kirkham was an RAF station!)

Despite such comfortable conditions, Kirkham Prison saw

more prisoners abscond during the period from 1998-2003 than any other open prison in England and Wales. A total of 911 inmates escaped during this period. Possibly as a result of this, in 2004 Kirkham Prison trialled an Intermittent Custody Scheme under which some inmates were released at weekends, whilst another set of prisoners were released from Monday till Friday. This arrangement was designed to allow short-term prisoners to remain in employment, independent housing, and maintain family ties during their jail term. (Certainly more 'cushy' than when we were 'prisoners of the RAF'). One fact that has emerged during my research is that my particular group of trainees must have been among the last, for the RAF vacated the station in December 1957.

Amongst the many accounts of incidents at RAF Kirkham is *Freckleton Air Disaster,* a poignant one written by George Fisher, a young aircrew navigator on attachment to No. 22 Aircrew Holding Unit at RAF Kirkham during the Second World War. He was billeted in the domestic site on the opposite side of the road to the main camp and often, for their morning break, he and several other aircrew members would eschew the NAAFI hut on camp and hurry down to the 'Sad Sack' café in nearby Freckleton village where they could enjoy a first-class 'cuppa.' Mr. and Mrs. Withers, the owners, also provided mouth-watering breakfasts, which were a great improvement on the ones supplied on camp.

On the morning of 23 August 1944, because he detested getting wet and a ferocious thunderstorm was in progress, he did not join four comrades at the café, but stayed on camp. As he made his way to the NAAFI the storm abated fleetingly and a break suddenly appeared in the clouds. In that brief moment he saw an American B24 Liberator aircraft before it disappeared into the clouds. At that time he was not aware that there were two such aircraft flying overhead in the storm, having recently taken off from a nearby base to undertake air tests.

Very shortly after this sighting, one of the pilots, got into difficulties whilst approaching the base, having been recalled, and crashed in the centre of Freckleton, with devastating results. The Sad Sack café was one of the buildings which caught the full impact and Mr. and Mrs. Withers and their daughter were amongst those who perished. Four civilians and several RAF and US airman were also killed.

George Fisher wrote, 'That night in my hut I was haunted by the sight of two empty beds in the corner and thanked the Lord for my aversion to heavy rain.'

Following the announcement of my posting my first task was to establish the whereabouts of RAF Tangmere. I discovered it was in Sussex, not far from Chichester. Thankful that the station was at least in England, although near to the south coast I realised that I had fared better than my friend Melvin who had been posted to the lonely north of Scotland outpost of Kinloss, situated near to the Moray Firth. Such thoughts were soon forgotten as I was looking forward to some welcome leave before reporting to my new station.

CHAPTER FOUR

Joining 34 Fighter Squadron at RAF Tangmere

Christmas was fast approaching as I arrived at RAF Tangmere, situated about three miles east of Chichester, a fighter airfield that had featured prominently in the Battle of Britain. My first task was to tour the station, visit every section and obtain a signature to note my arrival. It turned out to be a quite tortuous affair as I had not been shown around the station and knew no one. After going up many blind alleys I managed to collect enough signatures, but one episode was most chastening. It concerned my visit to the fire station, which was tucked away across the airfield from the main sections. It necessitated crossing the airfield whilst flying was in progress and I reckoned it was safest to walk around the perimeter track. Whilst doing this I had to cross the end of the runway and as I did so an officer leapt out of a hut nearby waving his arms and pointing frantically. I looked in the direction in which he was pointing to see to my horror an aircraft fast approaching as it was coming into land. I had been so wrapped up in my task, studying my partially completed card that I had been unaware of its presence. I high-tailed it away from the end of the runway, my heart pounding and hoping that I would not be taken to account for my stupidity. Thankfully, the officer returned to his hut and I heard no more about the incident.

I was informed that I would be joining the ground crew of 34 Squadron and be employed on first line servicing. This meant that I would carry out pre-flight and between-flight inspections of its Hawker Hunter aircraft, also do minor repairs to the fabric, refuelling and changing wheels when required. However, I was not allocated to the squadron initially as Christmas was looming and I was given menial tasks to perform, such as putting up the decorations in the airmen's dining hall and officers' mess in preparation for the forthcoming festivities. It is fortunate that I have a head for heights, for I was frequently teetering precariously on very high steps and my RAF career could have come to an abrupt end. Part of the celebrations was a Christmas Dinner, for which I still have the menu and serviette, complete with the RAF logo. An old-established RAF tradition was observed at the dinner, as it had been even in the dark days of intense conflict during the Second World War. The Station Commander assisted with the turkey carving and the sergeants were entertained in the Officers' Mess, following which, the officers and sergeants visited our dining hall and acted as waiters.

No one could complain of the fare, for it was well-cooked and enough to feed an army, or, should I say mob of hungry air force personnel. I will never forget that menu, which was as follows: tomato soup followed by turkey/roast pork and apple sauce, stuffing, chipolata sausages, croquet potatoes, Brussels sprouts and cauliflower. Pudding was Christmas pudding/mince pies, brandy sauce/custard, dessert of mixed nuts, and finally cheese and biscuits. This enormous meal was washed down with ales, stout, or fruit squash. As everyone was too bloated to move after it, we were treated to some hilarious entertainment, but there was more to come. The evening was rounded off by a dance, which proved very lively as there was plenty of female company for the airmen provided by a contingent of members of the WRAF (Women's Royal Air Force). This was most welcome after privations of Bridgnorth and Kirkham. It also yielded a little light relief from wondering what lay ahead in the New Year. Following the festivities I enjoyed several days' leave, the only drawback being the long journey to and from my home in Mansfield by train. I travelled via Chichester, Portsmouth, London and Nottingham, courtesy of my travel warrant and it seemed to take forever.

After the Christmas holiday it was time to return to Tangmere and 'earn my corn' doing what I had been trained to do. I was installed in 34 Fighter Squadron.

I felt quite miserable during the morning parade on my first day of 'action' as we stood in formation on the barrack square. It was raining and bitterly cold, a precursor to the rather unhappy seven weeks I was to spend at RAF Tangmere.

After the parade, the flight to which I been allocated proceeded onto the airfield, to our site of operations, a control cabin adjacent to a line of Hawker Hunter aircraft waiting at dispersal. I was immediately impressed by this row of fine machines at close quarters, with their sleek lines and attractive swept back wings. Apparently, I was not the only person to be impressed, for this excerpt from a glowing report by a pilot who flew the aircraft reads as follows: 'If there was ever an aircraft that displays a timeless shape and excellent aerodynamics, then the Hawker Hunter has to be the one. The aircraft handles just as Sir Sidney Camm's design intended. From testing the brakes during 'taxi-out' to applying full thrust at 50,000 feet plus, it is all there and flies like the thoroughbred that is the Hunter.' My first sight of this aircraft made me wish that I had taken a flying course, which would have been rather difficult to attain being a National Serviceman.

I followed the rest of my flight into the cabin and approached the desk used by the NCO's allocating the aircraft to the ground crew for inspection. I gave my name to a corporal behind the desk who informed me I would be assisting aircraftsman Hunt, who he called to the desk and introduced us to each other. 'Your pre-flight inspection is on 'L' for Lima,' he informed us. (All aircraft were identified by a letter prominently displayed on the aircraft.)

'Okay, corp.' said Hunt and led me from the cabin to one of the shining aircraft waiting on the tarmac. Airmen of various trades - engines, armourer, wireless and radar - were swarming over it.

Initially, we walked around the aircraft checking the fabric and looking for tiny cracks around the rivets. Wheels, tyres and undercarriage came next. Hunt advised that one of the most important checks was the depth of tread on the tyres, which was satisfactory on that occasion. 'If there is excessive wear the wheel has to be changed,' he said. At that moment a bowser (fuel tanker) arrived and Hunt began pull out the fuel pipe from it and attach the nozzle to the aircraft. As he did so he showed me how to lock it in position. 'Now you try,' he said as he removed the nozzle and handed it to me. I nearly dropped the pipe, it was so heavy, and I wrestled with the nozzle trying to locate it and lock it in position. Hunt laughed. 'Not easy is it, he commented, as I eventually managed to secure the nozzle. Finally we checked the compressed air system and hydraulics.

During the inspection I had naively suggested certain

procedures that we had been taught at Kirkham, to which Hunt replied, 'You don't need to do that.' Then and during those early days on the squadron I realised that much of what we learned during training was never used.

We returned to the control cabin to record the completed pre-flight check, which would be counter-signed by a corporal. The Flight Sergeant came up to us and told me that the NCO's performed routine checks on our activities as a matter of safety. 'So, don't think you can skimp your inspections or get away with sloppy maintenance,' he warned. From there we went into a nearby metal shelter, ('Al Tent' in RAF parlance), accompanied by the Flight Sergeant, where I was introduced to my fellow airmen. None of them appeared particularly friendly as they lounged inside the 'tin hut,' staring at me. The Flight Sergeant returned to the control cabin to await the arrival of the pilots.

Eventually, pilots began to appear and the Flight Sergeant stuck his head around the door of our shelter and shouted, 'Who's going to see the first three off?'(He was referring to the first three Hunters.) There was no movement by the airmen until the Flight Sergeant pointed at Hunt and two others, 'Right!' he said. 'You, you and you . . . get out there and take Plowright with you!' he demanded. The airmen he had indicated rose slowly and we left the hut. Not over-keen for work was the thought that crossed my mind.

A pilot was waiting beside 'L' for Lima as Hunt and I approached. 'Come on you chaps,' he said, 'I haven't got all day.' 'Sorry sir,' said Hunt. The three of us began a walk around the aircraft when the pilot noticed a pool of liquid on the ground. 'Is that hydraulic oil?' asked the pilot nervously. 'Oh no sir,' said Hunt, 'it's only water.' The pilot accepted this although I felt that the liquid should have been investigated, as it could be hydraulic oil (used for brakefluid, lowering and retracting the undercarriage and for operating other flight control mechanisms). I said nothing and we continued our tour, at the end of which the pilot climbed into the cockpit. Hunt climbed the steps, bent over the pilot and proceeded to fit his safety harness. When this was completed Hunt removed the steps and the pilot commenced his pre-flight checks which

Tangmere Airfield today

included testing the aircraft controls (moving the ailerons, flaps, trim tabs and rudder) and checking the various dials and warning devices. When this was complete he closed the cockpit canopy and the engine sprang into life. Hunt removed one of the chocks from the wheels and signalled for me to do the same and when this was completed the aircraft taxied away heading for the runway accompanied by the other two aircraft. At the end of the runway they awaited instructions from the control tower to take off. As 'L' for Lima did so Hunt crossed his fingers and grimaced, 'Hope our ruddy thing gets airborne, I don't know if it was water or hydraulic oil, but it's too late now.' If the pilot only knew the reaction of that airframe mechanic, I thought, but kept quiet. Hunt's fears were quelled when 'L' for Lima took off without a problem.

That day I accompanied Hunt on between-flight inspections and also observed other airframe mechanics as they went about theirs. When the aircraft returned from sorties members of the ground crew guided them from the perimeter track to their parked position at dispersal. This was done by arm waving, not with the aid of the 'table tennis bats' that you see used on film or television by civil aircraft ground crew.

A final inspection took place on the aircraft following their last sorties, after which the Hunters were towed back to their hangar. As our flight returned to our billet I realised that none of the other airmen apart from Hunt, the Flight Sergeant and the corporal had spoken to me that day.

I did overhear them talking about me some days later as I returned to the shelter and found the door open. I had been doing my own inspections and repairs for a few days and the gist of their conversation was that I was performing my duties slowly. Being new to the squadron I worked carefully and thoroughly, which must have upset some of the happy-go-lucky types.

I did not let on that I had heard their criticism and the shelter fell silent when I entered. I realised the critics were members of a clique that talked through pursed lips like gangsters and considered themselves to be 'hard cases.' This group, I found later were frequently in trouble both on camp and outside. One evening after a bout of hard drinking they caused considerable damage to property on their return to camp and were put in the guardroom. One of this bunch was a real pain who, despite having signed on as a regular and was receiving much higher pay, tried to borrow money from me to subsidise his drinking. I never forgot the incident and some years later I went to the cinema to see the film *Alfie*, the original one with Michael Caine in the lead role. Part way through the film Michael Caine entered a pub and approached a group at one of the tables. One of the group was sat with his back to Michael, who tapped him on the shoulder only for the man to stand up and tower over him. I could hardly believe my eyes, for it was the airman that had tried to borrow money from me! That was not the end of the affair as he also appeared in a James Bond film and in a long-running television advert.

During my period at RAF Tangmere I carried on with my mechanical engineering studies, this time at Portsmouth Technical College, as it was then. This involved travelling by bus to Portsmouth three evenings per week via Chichester. One such evening, I can always recall, I had just heard what I thought was wonderful news and it occupied my thoughts during the bus journeys to and from Portsmouth. A rumour was circulating around RAF Tangmere that the period of National Service was to be reduced from two years to eighteen months. As I was none too happy with the RAF at that time this really appealed to me. Unfortunately, the rumour was unfounded.

As Tangmere was so far from my home I was rarely able to take weekend leave and spent most weekends doing homework in the education centre on camp, which did not lighten my mood.

Some light relief was supplied by playing rugby for the station team, which entailed fixtures against local clubs in the area. It allowed time off for away matches and one such memorable away fixture was at Worthing, which meant a whole day away from the station. We travelled by coach, stopping at Arundel on the way and I remember admiring its stunning castle. What I cannot remember is the result of the match, but I can recall stopping for a post match celebration on the way back to camp. It was a rowdy and joyous affair with officers mixing convivially with airmen.

When we got back onto the coach I was seated next to a pilot from our squadron and we got into conversation. He was very talkative, probably due to the drink he had consumed, and was most forthcoming about his flying career. I eventually plucked up the courage to ask him something that had intrigued me for a while. 'How can you concentrate whilst flying an extremely expensive aircraft the morning after a late night or an enjoyable evening's drinking?' I inquired. He replied that you are concentrating so hard and applying yourself one hundred percent to the job in hand, you have no time for ill-effects. I still found it remarkable that he could cope with a hangover.

Other airmen volunteered for various sporting activities to get out of parades and enjoy time off. A friend of mine volunteered for the station boxing team, despite being unable to fight his way out of a paper bag! Weighing about nine stones wet through he nevertheless took a chance that he could attend training sessions but never be selected for the station team. Unfortunately for him, due to better boxers being unavailable through illness or being posted he was picked for the team. This resulted in nightmares and he became extremely nervous as the date of the inter-station boxing match drew near. Fortunately for him the event was postponed and when it finally took place a better boxer took his place. Uttering a huge sigh of relief he decided that parades and reporting for work each day was a safer option.

Another ruse to miss parades, as numbers were never checked, was to hide in your locker and hope that you were not discovered. This could only be tried by a few brave airmen until some were found hunched in their lockers, which resulted in head counts before parades.

CHAPTER FIVE

History of RAF Tangmere, including the High Speed Flight, the Schneider Trophy and the Suez Crisis

I mentioned that RAF Tangmere was in the thick of the action during the Battle of Britain in 1940, a period that has always fascinated me, so I decided to read up on its history. It was established in 1917, during the First World War, as a training station for the Royal Flying Corps. In early 1918 it was used by the United States Army Air Forces for training purposes until the end of the war, when it was temporarily closed. It reopened in 1925 as a base for the RAF's Fleet Air Arm and the following year it became equipped with Gloster Gamecocks belonging to 43 Squadron.

During the late 1930's, Hawker Furies, Gloster Gladiators and Hawker Hurricanes were based at Tangmere, powered by the famous Rolls Royce Merlin engines. In 1939 at the outbreak of the Second World War the airfield was enlarged to assist the defence of the south coast against attack by the German Luftwaffe.

By 1940 the first Supermarine Spitfire squadron had been formed at a satellite airfield at nearby Westhampnett at the outset of the Battle of Britain. Due to its position guarding the south coast, Tangmere became one of the prime targets for the Luftwaffe during its attacks on RAF airfields. The most damaging raid on the airfield occurred in August of that year when 100 Junkers Stuka dive-bombers and fighters crossed the coast and most headed for Tangmere. At the time of this attack, Winston Churchill, the Prime Minister, was at Fighter Command Headquarters at Bentley Priory with Air Marshall Hugh Dowding, AOC Fighter Command, observing the progress of the RAF against numerous enemy bombing raids. By evening 75 German aircraft had been shot down, a telling blow to the invincibility of the Luftwaffe, who called it 'Black Thursday.' Fighter command, to its credit, lost only 30 aircraft. When Churchill left Dowding's headquarters that evening, he described the day's conflict as 'One of the greatest days in history.'

However, Tangmere had suffered badly in the attack with many aircraft wrecked or damaged on the ground, in addition to the destruction of World War One hangars and other buildings. Fourteen RAF personnel and six civilians were killed and there were many others injured. Despite the setback the station carried on and was soon brought back into full operation.

Tangmere had 'earned its stripes' and it continued to play an important role within the RAF 11 Group that covered the vital south-east area of England. The legless fighter ace, Douglas Bader, a hero of mine, was based at Tangmere in 1941 as a Wing Commander. I was lucky enough to catch sight of him during my service, more of which later.

One of the first American pilots to be killed in the Second World War, Billy Fiske, flew from Tangmere, whilst serving in the RAF. He was the 1928 and 1932 Olympic champion bobsled driver, who became the youngest gold medalist in any winter sport (aged sixteen), until surpassed by Toni Nieminen after an interval of many years (1992). At the Winter Olympics of 1932 Billy was given the honour of carrying the flag for the United States at the opening ceremony. He was selected for, but declined to lead, the bobsled team in the 1936 Winter Olympics in Germany. Some said at the time this was due to his opposition to German politics and it may explain his decision to join the war effort in 1940. As an American citizen he willingly 'pledged his life and loyalty to the king, George VI,' for which he paid with his life. In 1940 he joined 601 Squadron at Tangmere, nicknamed 'The Millionaires' Squadron.' Flying a Hurricane, in the thick of the action during the Battle of Britain, Billy received a bullet through his fuel tank. Despite burns to his hands and ankles and his aircraft badly damaged, he nursed his Hurricane home, just making it by gliding over a hedgerow and onto the airfield. Although he landed safely he had to be assisted from the aircraft and shortly afterwards his fuel tank exploded. Billy was admitted to hospital in Chichester but died forty-eight hours later. He was 29 years old.

On 4 July 1941, a plaque was unveiled in the crypt of St. Paul's Cathedral with the following inscription: *An American citizen who died that England might live.* The decision to unveil this plaque on American Independence Day was most

RAF Tangmere – Two Hurricanes in a low-level pass over the airfield

likely a political one. The United States had not officially entered the war and Winston Churchill was very keen to popularise Billy's sacrifice and to encourage them to do so.

Another hero named Billy was attached to Tangmere during the Battle of Britain. He was Group Captain Billy Drake, who became a fighter ace, shooting down twenty enemy aircraft, plus six probable kills and nine damaged. He flew Hurricanes, Spitfires and Curtiss P-40's (Tomahawks and Kittyhawks) with squadrons based in England, France, West Africa, North Africa and Malta and became the top-scoring RAF P-40 pilot. Billy joined 1 Squadron at Tangmere in 1937, flying the Hawker Fury before converting to the Hurricane. Following the outbreak of war the squadron was posted to France and during the Battle of France (April 1940) Drake registered his first kill. Other victories in the sky above France included a German Dornier and a Heinkel. Whilst in combat with another Dornier, Billy was shot down by a Messerschmitt 109 and received shell splinters in his back, but managed to bail out of his blazing Hurricane. This ended his participation in that campaign.

RAF Tangmere – Pilots of 65 Squadron gather round a Spitfire

Some months later, when Billy had recovered from his injuries, he returned to operational duty at Tangmere, with 213 Squadron. Promoted to Flight Lieutenant, he flew Spitfires on specialised low-level reconnaissance over the Channel and the French coast. He claimed a further two kills and two probables. In recognition of his actions he was awarded the DFC (Distinguished Flying Cross) in 1941.

In December of that year he was sent to West Africa to form and command 128 Squadron in Sierra Leone. Whilst there, he shot down a Vichy French Glenn Martin bomber, near Freetown. Seemingly, always on the move, he was posted to Air Headquarters Middle East and then on to RAF Gambut in Egypt where he commanded 112 Squadron, flying P-40's. During his time there he shot down two Junkers Ju87s.

More decorations and promotion followed as Billy scored a further thirteen kills. He was awarded a Bar to his DFC in July 1942 and five months later the DSO (Distinguished Service Order). In January 1942 he reached the rank of Wing Commander and was sent to command a Wing at RAF Krendi in Malta.

Before the year was over he was back in England (was he the most mobile RAF officer of the Second World War!). Now he was commanding 20 Wing, operating Hawker Typhoons together with the United States Second Tactical Air Force. It was not long before he was on the move once more, for he was sent on liaison duties to Fort Leavenworth in the United States where he was awarded the American Distinguished Flying Cross.

Returning once more to England he acted as Deputy Station Commander at RAF Biggin Hill and finished the Second World War as a staff officer at Supreme Headquarters Allied Expeditionary Force.

Later, Billy served as a staff officer and air attaché at operational headquarters in Japan and Singapore. His real love was the fighter environment and he was sent to the Fighter Leader school as an instructor in 1949, having been previously employed in training pilots during the Second World War as Chief Flying Instructor at RAF Llandow.

Then he was posted to Switzerland, which was fortuitous, for his passion was skiing, having earlier captained the RAF ski team. He remained there until 1962 when he returned to England before retiring from the RAF as Group Captain in 1963. He was held in high regard during his years in the RAF as one of the most colourful and skilled fighter pilots and as someone who led by example, like Douglas Bader, and inspired all those who flew with him. He lived to the ripe old age of ninety-four and died only a short time ago in August 2001.

As a footnote to his remarkable career in the RAF, it should be mentioned that Billy was credited with half a kill amongst his many. Another pilot was given the other half!

A little known fact concerning Tangmere is that it became a secret base during the Second World War for the Special Operations Executive (SOE) set up on the orders of Winston Churchill and Minister of Economic Warfare, Hugh Dalton. This organization flew British agents to and from France and conducted guerilla warfare against the Axis powers. It also instructed and aided local resistance movements and assisted espionage, sabotage and reconnaissance behind enemy lines. Churchill ordered the SOE to 'set Europe ablaze.' In the event of a German invasion of Britain it would serve as the core of a British resistance movement. Few people knew of its existence and it was known as 'Churchill's Secret Army.'

Its main transmitting and receiving stations in Britain were situated in Buckinghamshire, near to Bletchley Park, that housed the famous code-breaking unit. The organisation employed or controlled over 13,000 people, of whom around 3,200 were women and a considerable number of these brave individuals lost their lives. Today a commemorative plaque adorns a wall of Tangmere Cottage, which stands close to the main gate of the airfield, as a tribute to the SOE who used it throughout the war.

In early 1940 two nearby bombing decoys were built to deflect German bombing from Tangmere airfield. The daytime decoy consisted of a replica airfield equipped with dummy Hawker Hurricanes and at night-time a pattern of lights was used, which, when seen from the air, resembled a real airfield. I have no information regarding the effectiveness of these dummy sites, but the idea was a sound one.

After the war, in 1946, the RAF High Speed Flight was re-formed in an attempt to break the world air speed record. It operated from Tangmere as part of Central Fighter Establishment, an RAF formation that dealt with the development of fighter aircraft tactics, tested new fighter aircraft and trained squadron and flight commanders. The High Speed Flight was commanded by Group Captain E.M. Donaldson, DSO, DFC and two Gloster Meteor IV's were prepared for the record attempt. In September of that year a new world record of 616 miles per hour was set by Group Captain 'Teddy' Mortlock-Donaldson over a three-kilometre course between Littlehampton and Worthing. A few years later, in 1953, Squadron Leader Neville Duke attained a speed of 727 miles per hour.

The High Speed Flight was originally formed for the purpose of competing in the 1927 race for the Schneider Trophy to be held in Italy. The trophy was a competition for seaplanes initiated by Jacques Schneider a financier, balloonist and aircraft enthusiast, in 1911. A prize of £1,000 was offered to the winner. It was meant to encourage technical advances in civil

A Supermarine S.5 that won the Schneider Trophy race in 1927

aviation, but became a contest of pure speed, though very significant in advancing aeroplane design. The race was actually held eleven times between 1913 and 1931 and it proved very popular, sometimes drawing crowds of over 2,000 spectators.

Six aircraft were taken to Venice for the 1927 race – two Supermarine S.5's, three Gloster IV's and a single Short Crusader. The latter was slower than the rest and was merely intended for training, but, unfortunately, it crashed. The Supermarine S.5's came first and second, with neither the Gloster nor the three Italian aircraft completing the race. The High Speed Flight was disbanded after the race as the Air Ministry objected to the use of serving pilots. This problem was, however, resolved and the Flight reformed. In 1928 Samuel Kinkade made an attempt on the air speed record in a Supermarine S.5, but at the approach to the start of the course the aircraft plunged into the water and the pilot was killed.

The 1929 Trophy race was held at Cowes, having now become biennial and Britain, being the previous winner, played host to the contest. Rolls Royce had now developed a

BRITISH TEAM FOR SCHNEIDER TROPHY RACE, 1929.

The British team for the Schneider Trophy race in 1929

supercharged engine, which gave Supermarine's designer R.J. Mitchell, of Spitfire fame, far more power for his new Supermarine S.6, which won the race. Mitchell designed several Schneider Trophy winning seaplanes before producing his finest aircraft, the Supermarine Spitfire, which still inspires boys from the ages of eight to eighty!

In 1931 it seemed that the British would not raise a team, for the Cabinet vetoed RAF involvement and Government funding. The public would have none of this and backed the idea of a national team. A wealthy benefactor, shipping heiress, Lady Lucy Houston, offered to pay £100,000 towards the cost. This was accepted by the Government and the RAF was allowed to compete. However, the race was an anti-climax, for no other country entered a team. All that was required was for one of the Flight's aircraft to complete the course, so the plan was to beat the previous winning time of 1929 and then to go all-out for a new record. The first goal was met according to plan – Flight Lieutenant Bootham winning at 340 mph, 12mph faster than the 1929 time. The world record was then achieved by Flight Lieutenant Stainforth at 407 mph, the first person to travel faster than 400 mph.

Under the rules of the Schneider Trophy, a third win became an outright win in perpetuity and having thus completed three consecutive victories the British retained the trophy and the race was discontinued until 1981 when it was revived by the Royal Aero Club and opened on a handicap basis to any propeller-driven land plane capable of maintaining 100 mph in straight and level flight.

The race continues to this day and, although the venue has varied it is flown on most occasions around the Solent. Since 1977 the trophy has been entrusted to the Royal Aero Club and is on display at the Science Museum in London. However, a replica has been cast for presentation purposes.

In 1955, No.1 Squadron at Tangmere was newly equipped with the aircraft I would eventually work on, the Hawker Hunter. When the Suez Crisis began in 1956 a Tangmere wing of twenty-five Hunters was deployed in Cyprus for five months on air defence duties. Egyptian President Abdul Nasser had nationalised and seized control of the Suez Canal, a vital conduit for oil. By blocking the flow, Nasser planned to cripple the British economy at the time of the Cold War, when Britain and France were struggling to maintain their influence in the Middle East and North Africa. Britain still had an Empire, but some countries had already left and it was battling to put down revolts and uprisings. In Cyprus a British Minister announced that the island 'could never be independent.'

The British Prime Minister at that time was Anthony Eden who had been brought up politically in the 1930's and was against appeasement. He could not accept that Egypt should run the Suez Canal and was alarmed when Nasser announced that he was nationalising the Suez Canal Company (partly, he said, to pay for the Aswan dam that the West had refused to finance).

This announcement caused Eden to hatch a secret tripartite plot with France and Israel. France was hostile to Nasser because Egypt was helping the Algerian rebels and Israel was wishing to have revenge for Palestinian attacks and the Egyptian blockade of the Straits of Tiran. The idea was that Israel would attack Egypt across the Sinai Peninsula. Britain and France would then issue an ultimatum to both countries to stop fighting, or they would intervene to 'protect' the canal.

President Eisenhower, concerned about wider relations with the Arab world, was horrified at such a venture, but the plan went ahead. Once Israel invades Egypt, Britain and France take on their guise as peacemakers and begin bombing Egyptian positions. France and Britain are condemned at the United Nations and the Western Alliance is badly damaged. The Americans tell Britain to evacuate promptly and, with no backing from the enraged United Nations, Britain begins to do so. A UN peace-keeping force is formed and within two weeks advance units arrive in Egypt. Bowing to international pressure and the arrival of the UN force, British and French forces complete their withdrawal from Egypt by the end of 1956 and Israel withdraws in the spring of 1957.

The whole debacle did great damage to Britain's prestige, virtually ended Eden's career and represented the end of a long period of British imperial history. I do not know if the Tangmere Wing of Hunters took part in the conflict. If not, I am sure a close eye was kept on proceedings in Egypt by the RAF.

The advent of 1958 brought my short period of duty at Tangmere to an end and by February of that year I was on the move once more, the reason being 34 Squadron was being disbanded, yet again. The squadron had quite a chequered history, having come into existence as long ago as 1916 during the First World War. It was posted to France that year as a reconnaissance unit and was then transferred to the Italian front in 1917 where it flew reconnaissance aircraft and bombers until the end of the war. In 1919 the squadron was disbanded and it was not until 1935 that it reformed, initially flying Hawker Hinds then Bristol Blenheims. Before the start of World War Two it was sent to Singapore and when Japan entered the war 34 Squadron suffered such heavy losses it was decimated and the few aircraft that remained were transferred to India. It was re-formed once more in 1942 and carried out bombing raids on Japanese bases in Burma until it was re-equipped with Hurricanes before switching to P-47 Thunderbolts in the latter stages of the war. In October 1945 the squadron was disbanded again.

Tangmere Memorial

Between 1946 and 1952 it was re-formed and disbanded twice, finally arriving at Tangmere in 1954 when it was re-formed flying Gloster Meteors, re-equipping with Hawker Hunters in 1955.

I was informed that I was being transferred, along with another airman, to another fighter squadron. RAF Tangmere managed to struggle on without me until 1970 when it closed and a lone spitfire flew over the airfield in salute as the RAF ensign was lowered.

Following the closure some of the land around the runways was returned to farming. Tangmere Airfield Nurseries purchased part of the airfield and erected huge greenhouses for the cultivation of peppers and aubergines, amongst more regular produce. Today the company has a very professional website advertising itself as a Commercial Pepper Grower and Packer. Its biologically controlled crop allows customers to receive a reliable and continuous supply of top quality sweet peppers all year round.

Meanwhile Father Time worked his wicked ways and until 1983 thirty-seven acres of the site, housing barracks, administration blocks and repair workshops were left derelict until purchased by Seawards Homes and many of the other RAF buildings were demolished. The officers' quarters were retained as homes and housing spread over the airfield. A few of the original RAF buildings remain, including the original RAF hangars and the World War Two control tower that is due for restoration. Sections of the runways and perimeter track are still to be seen.

To return to my story, my fellow airman and I were each given a travel warrant that indicated our new posting was within easy reach of Cambridge. Following several train and bus journeys on a cold winter's day we arrived at RAF Duxford well after dark. It took some getting to know my new surrounding during that evening, but the following morning I awoke to discover that I would join the ground crew of 65 Squadron that was also equipped with Hawker Hunters, which was good news.

CHAPTER SIX

Life on 65 Fighter Squadron at RAF Duxford, including the Jordan Crisis, the EOKA Campaign in Cyprus and the Munich Air Crash

Thus began a much more pleasant period of my service, which was to last until I was demobbed. I fitted in well with my new squadron that I came to know as the 'Sixty-Fifth Foot and Mouth!' Shortly after my transfer from Tangmere I was promoted to the exultant rank of LAC (Leading Aircraftsman) which meant a rise in pay of a few shillings per week.

RAF Duxford, I discovered, was heavily involved throughout the Second World War, particularly during the Battle of Britain. On my arrival I was pleased to see two squadrons based there, the aforementioned 65 Squadron and its neighbour, 64 Squadron, equipped with Gloster Javelins.

The Javelin was born out of an Air Ministry requirement for a high-performance night fighter. It had a distinctive appearance, quite different to the Hawker Hunter. Its broad delta wings were complimented by a high finned 'T' tail and it was capable of speeds up to 710 mph. During the aircraft's initial trials it had an unfortunate series of crashes and design faults, which resulted in a lengthy period of testing and modification. It first flew in 1951 but the first Javelins were not delivered to the RAF until 1956. Three test pilots were killed during this period and a fourth, although experiencing major problems managed to land his aircraft. The elevator surfaces had become detached, making the aircraft uncontrollable and it caught fire on landing. The pilot was awarded the George Medal for his gallant action and for retrieving vital flight data from the burning aircraft.

At its peak, during 1959 to 1962, the Javelin was operational on fourteen RAF squadrons. After this time the numbers dropped dramatically and by 1964 only four squadrons were equipped with the aircraft. The closest the RAF Javelins came to combat was during the Malayan confrontation with Indonesia (1963/1966) when combat patrols were flown from RAF Tengah over the jungles of Malaysia. During that period an Indonesian Air Force Lockheed Hercules crashed whilst

A Gloster Javelin

trying to evade interception by a Javelin.

The last aircraft of this type was withdrawn from service in 1968, but one Javelin carried on flying with the Aeroplane and Armament Experimental Establishment at Boscombe Down until 1975.

During my time at dispersal at Tangmere it had dawned on me that being new and over-eager, I had been volunteering to 'see aircraft in and off' and do pre-flight and between-flight inspections on a regular basis. I realised that I was the only one doing so, whilst the other ground crew members hung back until chastised by the Flight Sergeants. The same situation applied at Duxford, but, being wiser I did not move until my name was called and work was delegated. I clearly recall one of the sergeants allocating the tasks was frequently hung over in a morning, having drunk too freely in the Sergeant's Mess the previous evening. However, he was a very fair and pleasant man and the ground crew overlooked his lapses. One of these related to the occasion when a corporal, having just checked on the work done by the ground crew during a pre-flight inspection, entered the control cabin and said to this particular sergeant, 'T for Tommy, T for Tango completed.' The sergeant, still a little woolly-headed, thought he was referring to two aircraft and rang through to the flight office with that fact, having been confused by the two call-signs he had been given for the same aircraft.

The work was not too onerous and one bonus was being on the airfield in the fresh air most of the time, albeit sometimes in bad weather, in a tent. I had grown used to the routine, which was enlivened at times with some memorable occurrences. Part of my responsibility was the examination of the engine blades at a fixed frequency, a job that I disliked. It involved squirming through the air intakes (openings in the root of the wings) to access the engine nacelle - the outer casing of the engine - in order to inspect the state of the blades. On one occasion I had struggled into the claustrophobic confines and was duly carrying out my inspection when I heard the click of a switch in the cockpit above me. Convinced it could be a fitter (engine mechanic) about to switch on the engine for a test, I was out of that aircraft's innards in record time. Thankfully, it turned out not to be the case and these were the days before the tightening of Health and Safety regulations. Today, there would be warning notices posted, the engine control switch in the cockpit locked in the 'off' position and an airman standing guard whilst I undertook such a dangerous checking procedure.

Another health and safety hazard was created whilst an airframe mechanic was helping to remove an ejector seat from an aircraft that had been put aside for maintenance. The seat had to be removed in order to gain access to a component and as it was being lifted from the cockpit the drogue gun inadvertently fired. This device is mounted on the side of the ejector seat and when it is operated a rod shoots from its housing pulling a small stabilising parachute behind it that opens prior to the main parachute. Due to an error the drogue gun cartridge had not been disarmed by an armourer and the oversight had not been discovered by the corporal armourer who signed off the device as being safe.

As the airframe mechanic was leaning over the side of the cockpit removing the seat the rod activated and hit him in the chest at great velocity. That airman was the luckiest man alive, for the rod, which could penetrate right through your body, miraculously struck a tyre pressure gauge in the breast pocket of the mechanic's overalls and was deflected. He was taken to hospital but he had escaped serious injury, or worse. However, the tyre pressure gauge was seriously bent!

In addition to the Hunters and Javelins the station had two old aircraft that were still airworthy. One of them was a Meteor, to which I referred in an earlier chapter, which was used for towing a banner that acted as a target during air-firing exercises. It was probably the remaining remnant of the Meteors of 64 and 65 Squadrons that were based here in the early 1950's. Another fact that I discovered was that Meteors scored their first combat success during the Second World War. In 1944 a Meteor of 616 Squadron destroyed two flying bombs over London.

The other aeroplane was a deHavilland Vampire, a twin-boomed fighter/bomber. It was a twin-seater aircraft used for training that we christened the 'Screaming Spoon,' because of the high-pitched sound of its engine. We had no need to look skywards at the returning aircraft, for its distinctive sound could be heard from a great distance.

Talking of air-firing exercises, reminds me of the excitement it generated amongst the pilots of our squadron. There was keen competition to obtain the highest number of 'kills,' but I am ashamed to say it did not inspire the same thrill amongst the ground crew, to whom it was just another working day. We had an American pilot attached to our squadron for a period who was very keen to impress. On returning from an air-firing sortie he virtually jumped from his aircraft shouting, 'I got four! … I got four!' meaning he had shot down the equivalent number of aircraft during the exercise. If the man expected a rapturous welcome from the ground crew on hearing this news he was sadly disappointed, for he was greeted with deafening silence and indifference.

I had the dubious pleasure of meeting another American pilot, flying a Hawker Hunter, who had been diverted overnight to Duxford because of bad weather. I was assigned to 'see him off' the following day and in so doing received quite a shock. He turned up in 'civvies' (ordinary clothes) carrying a heavy travelling bag and with a cigar stub stuck in the corner of his mouth, unlit thankfully. He clambered quickly into the cockpit without inspecting the aircraft and dumped the bag between his knees. As I bent over him to fasten his safety harness he uttered the immortal words, 'Let's get to goddam hell outa' here!' He revved up the aircraft's engine and I removed the steps hurriedly before he sped from dispersal as though chased by the 'hounds of hell.'

I was left pondering the fact that our pilots wore all the safety gear, including pressure suits and helmets and here was this Yank acting as though flying was a mere walk in the park. Thankfully, his aircraft took off without incident, to, I know not where. I had a mental picture of him being in such a hurry to get back to his homeland, his aircraft ran out of fuel and ditched in the Atlantic Ocean!

Other Hawker Hunters were diverted to Duxford on another occasion, but this was an exciting affair. The pilots were members of the 'Black Arrows,' the forerunners of the 'Red Arrows' aerobatics team, which was formed in 1955 from 111 Squadron based at RAF North Weald. They were admired for their daring displays, particularly for their trademark formation of sixteen Hawker Hunters flying in unison, arranged in a diamond shape.

The Black Arrows originally consisted of an unofficial group of four Gloster Meteors that in 1956 was changed to five Hawker Hunters that received official recognition as an aerobatic team. Their name was created at the Paris Air Show in 1957 when a French journalist referred to the team as resembling black arrows, with their swept back wings and dark colouring. The following year, 1958, the team increased to nine aircraft and, during the demonstration week of the Farnborough Air Show, they performed 'loop and roll' in a formation of twenty-two Hunters, which is a long-standing record.

Consequently, it was quite an honour to meet the pilots and to 'see them off' in their distinctive black aircraft. Unfortunately, they did not give us an aerobatic display before leaving.

In September 1958 Duxford played host to three Hawker Hunter squadrons from other airfields for a period of one week. Along with 65 Squadron they were due to take part in a fly-past over Farnborough airfield to commemorate the anniversary of the Battle of Britain (15 September 1940). The weekdays were used for practicing formation flying and Saturday was to be the day of the fly-past at the Farnborough Air Show, the one at which the twenty-two Hunters performed their aerobatics.

With pilots from other squadrons being unused to Duxford airfield there was frequent over-shooting of the runway when aircraft returned from practice. This did not go down at all well with the local farmer into whose field the aircraft trundled. Unfortunately, these occurrences were nothing compared to a disaster towards the end of the week when one of the visiting aircraft crashed on take-off. They were taking off in pairs and the pilot of the one involved made a fatal error (I think regarding the setting of a trim tab) that caused it to flip over and crash in the poor farmer's field.

Some of the ground crew, including me, were ordered to the scene to search for debris from the stricken aircraft. The fuselage was more or less intact, but still smouldering from the heat and the foam that had been sprayed on it and wreckage was spread over a wide area. The pilot, who was still strapped into the ejector seat, would obviously have known nothing after the impact. It was a very disconsolate group of airmen who trudged around the field on a gruesome search.

During my service with 65 Squadron I was lucky enough to enjoy several trips to other airfields along with other crew members on air-firing detachment. A small number of aircraft were involved and it made a pleasant change to carry out my duties in different locations. The first of these short detachments was spent at RAF Odiham, in Hampshire, along with three Hawker Hunters and a small ground crew. I was fortunate to go by air, in an Avro Anson, an aircraft that had given stout service during World War II. The Anson was designed as a twin-engine, multi-roll aircraft and earned the nickname 'Faithful Annie,' by serving the RAF from 1934 to 1968. It was named after Admiral George Anson a key figure in the mid-eighteenth century Royal Navy, who famously navigated the world between1740 and 1744. He was Admiral of the Fleet and a wealthy aristocrat that commanded the Navy during the Seven Years War which lasted from 1756 to 1763. Britain emerged from the war as the world's leading colonial power, having gained a number of new territories at the Treaty of Paris.

The Anson was originally intended for maritime reconnaissance, but was used mainly for air crew training and for light transport. At the beginning of the Second World War, twenty-six RAF squadrons were operating the Anson within Coastal and Bomber Command. Early in the conflict an Anson scored a probable hit on a German U boat. In June 1940 three Ansons were attacked by nine Messerschmitts. Remarkably, the Ansons shot down two of the German aircraft and damaged a third before the 'dogfight' ended, without losing any of their own. Also in 1940 two Ansons from No. 2 Flying Training School collided in mid-air and became locked together. Miraculously, they made a successful emergency landing.

RAF Odiham, a fighter station at the time of my visit, is situated a little to the south of the historic village of Odiham in Hampshire. It boasts a once impressive castle, now in ruins and a former royal palace. The castle was built by King John in 1204, its position due to the fact that it lay midway between Winchester and Windsor.

I spent three enjoyable days at the RAF station that was opened as a permanent airfield in 1937 by, would you believe, Erhard Milch, Chief of Staff for the Luftwaffe? What an ironic choice! During the Second World War American P-51 Mustangs and Hawker Typhoons were based there. After the D Day landings the base became a prisoner of war camp until RAF Fighter Command took over the former airfield. During the immediate post-war period Spitfires, Vampires and Meteors operated from the base. In 1953 the newly-crowned Elizabeth II visited the station as part of the celebrations of her coronation.

Hunters and Javelins replaced the early jet fighter planes and these were followed by Chinook HC helicopters, including the HC3 Type that had remained in storage for eight years because of certification problems regarding navigation and communications systems (avionics). It was 2010 before the helicopters were fitted with HC2 avionics to allow them to enter service with the RAF. In 2011 six personnel from RAF Odiham were honoured for their gallantry during the Afghanistan conflict.

My next detachment was to RAF Horsham St. Faith, situated a mere few miles from Norwich, a historic city with a selection of fine buildings. Despite being on the station for only a few days I managed to visit the city that I discovered has been important since the Norman Conquest. The preservation of its buildings seems of prime concern to the local authority in recent times and its different architectural styles complement, rather than detract from, each other. It was a particular pleasure to walk through the Royal Arcade that has a most attractive façade and runs from Gentleman's Walk to Back of the Inns.

Norwich possesses a thriving market and a splendid Norman Cathedral. In the spacious surrounds of Cathedral Close I found many medieval properties. During my walk around the city I visited Strangers Hall, its earliest sections dating from around 1320, which is now a museum. Strangers Hall derives its name from its association with Flemish weavers, who were encouraged to settle in Norwich in the sixteenth century in order to revitalise the textile industry, which had prospered during the fourteenth century.

I stopped to admire the splendid castle, built by the Normans as a palace around 900 years ago. From the fourteenth century it was used as a prison until it became a museum in 1894. In fact, Norwich appears rich in museums because it also possesses Bridewell Museum, a former merchant's house dating from 1825. Later it also became a prison for tramps and women (a bridewell), before changing to a museum.

The airfield itself opened in 1940 as a bomber station. The first fighter aircraft to operate from there were Spitfires of 19 and 66 Squadrons, transferred from Duxford. During those early days of the war the station received a visit from the then Prime Minister, Neville Chamberlain and General Sir Alan Brooke.

In 1941 an aircraft from 18 Squadron, operating from Horsham St. Faith, en route to attack a power station at Gosnay in France, dropped a box by parachute over the airfield at St. Omer Longeunesse containing a spare leg for Wing Commander Douglas Bader who had been shot down over France and lost one of his artificial legs in the process! The United States Army Air Forces used the station in

ROYAL AIR FORCE PASSENGER RAILWAY WARRANT.		R.A.F. Form 413
Fare Not Payable at Time of Booking.		(Revised June, 1956)

STAMP **H. Q.** OF

C 600737

4 JUN 1958

R.A.F. DUXFORD UNIT

CHARGES PAYABLE BY :—
The Under Secretary of State,
Air Ministry (F.3(c))
London Road,
Stanmore,
Middlesex.

TO THE BRITISH TRANSPORT COMMISSION ... 4 / 6 /19 58

OR ... CONCERN(?)

Please issue, without charge to bearer, tickets as under, VIA THE RECOGNISED DIRECT AND CHEAPEST ROUTE.

NUMBER OF PASSENGERS (IN WORDS)

	FIRST	SECOND
ADULTS		ONE
CHILDREN AGED 3 AND UNDER 14		
FROM	WHITTLESFORD	
TO	LETCHWORTH	SINGLE/RETURN *

THIS WARRANT IS NOT TRANS-FERABLE, IS AVAILABLE FOR 30 DAYS FROM DAY OF ISSUE AND MUST BE EXCHANGED FOR TICKETS AT THE BOOKING OFFICE WHERE THE JOURNEY IS AUTHORISED TO COMMENCE.

Any alteration to this Warrant must be signed by a responsible Officer and supported by the Unit stamp.

No entry is to be made for children under 3 years of age.

Particulars of No. 5043445 Rank SAC
Bearer † Name PLOWRIGHT
If issued for Service
Family state husband's Rank — Number —
Authority for Journey D.R. 2490
Reason for Journey EDUCATION
Chargeable against A.F.
Signature of Issuing Officer ...
Rank ... Unit DUXFORD

TO BE COMPLETED BY THE BOOKING CLERK						
Date	Route	Description of Tickets	Nos. of Tickets	£	s.	d.

*Delete as †Person in charge of party. Service numbers, names and ranks (or status) of necessary. the remainder of the party with ages of any children must be entered overleaf.

Railway Warrant for travel to Letchworth College

1942, flying the B 26 Marauder medium bomber. The unit stayed for two months until re-assigned to North Africa.

My third and final detachment in this country, during May 1958, was to RAF Leuchars near St. Andrews, in Fife, home of the famous golf course. The airfield lies on the coast and the runway nearly extends onto the beach. It was fascinating watching the aircraft taking off and wondering if I would witness a repeat of the over-shooting of the Duxford runway. Thankfully, there were no such incidents. When the wind direction dictated that the aircraft take off and land towards the sea, had there been any misjudgments, the pilots concerned may have endured a soaking!

During the detachment there was no weekend flying and to keep the pilots and ground crew of our party entertained, a coach trip to Edinburgh was arranged. Having never visited that appealing city at that time, it turned out to be a very interesting affair, which included a visit to its famous castle and a stroll along bustling Princes Street. An amusing incident occurred on our return journey as the coach driver, who was unfamiliar with the region, lost his way and drove along a very narrow road before ending up in a farmyard. It was a very puzzled farmer who encountered a coach party outside his back door. At least he had a sense of humour, for he said if we had come to help with the harvest, we were too early!

I mentioned earlier that I carried on my engineering studies during my National Service and that I attended three technical colleges during my two years. I was fortunate to be given day release to study at Letchworth Technical College during my time at Duxford. Instead of the previous three evenings per week I had endured at Preston and Portsmouth, I had each Thursday free to cycle the sixteen miles to Letchworth (having brought my bicycle to the camp) for the rest of my service. This arrangement did not go down well with some of my ground crew who asked why I should be given one day per week off. I suggested that they could have the same opportunity if they cared to study for qualifications. However, I volunteered to return to work after my return from Letchworth on days when flying lasted through late afternoon and early evening. After several stints of working on the aircraft after a day of study the

*A party of 65 Squadron ground crew waiting to board a
Blackburn Beverley en route for Cyprus*

opposition ceased as they saw that I was not 'skiving off.'

The end of my first year HNC course coincided with the two-week detachment to RAF Leuchars and I had requested to remain at Duxford to sit the required examinations. This was rejected and it was arranged for me to sit them at Leuchars with the Education Officer acting as invigilator. Consequently, I spent my evenings there swotting for the exams and the final day sitting them. I do not know who arranged for the examination papers to be sent to Leuchars, but I was indebted to the RAF and Letchworth Technical College for being so amenable. I managed to pass all three of the exams and looked forward to taking the final year of the course in the RAF, for my period of service did not end until the following May.

A pleasant surprise awaited me on my return to Duxford, I received another promotion, to the rank of SAC (Senior Aircraftsman) and a further increase in pay.

What should have been my longest detachment with 65 Squadron took place in October 1958 at which time three RAF squadrons were being kept on standby in Cyprus for a period

A campsite at RAF Nicosia

of three months.

Political turmoil was occurring in the Middle East, with trouble in Jordan, Lebanon, Iraq and the EOKA terrorist organisation active in Cyprus.

The Jordan crisis of July 1958 was probably the single emergency in King Hussein's perilous career in whose timing he had no part and it possibly brought him to the brink of abdication. He had acted quickly and decisively to other crises. For example, the coup attempt in 1957 and the one initiated by Black September, a Palestinian paramilitary organisation, named after their attempt to topple him in September 1970. This was rebuffed by the king declaring military rule.

The 1958 Baghdad revolution, which saw the end of the monarchy in Iraq and the death of King Faisal II, came as a shock to Hussein, and Jordan was isolated as never before. Hussain reacted by seeking help from the United States and Britain. In July 1958 Britain flew troops into Amman to try and stabalise the regime. For some weeks the political atmosphere in Jordan was explosive, but martial law kept order and the army stayed loyal to Hussein.

To add to the mix, Lebanon was threatened by a civil war between Maronite Christians and Muslims and the United States became involved, following a request for assistance by its president, and sent troops into Beirut.

It was in the light of these events that the RAF were on standby in Cyprus and, although we did not know it at the time the revolutions, particularly the one in Iraq, marked a watershed in the history of the Middle East and the region's relations with the West. They represented the overthrow of the old order and the virtual end of the British Empire in the Middle East, even though the British presence continued in the Gulf and Aden. The crises also marked the ascendancy of the United States as a Middle East power, taking the place of Britain.

Our Squadron was given orders to prepare to fly to Nicosia for a three-month stint and preparations began. Initially, vehicles, equipment and a small team was dispatched in several Blackburn Beverleys, heavy transport aircraft flown by squadrons of RAF Coastal Command. These massive beasts were the largest planes supplied to the RAF and were designed to carry huge, bulky loads and land them on rough or imperfect runways, or even on dirt strips. They even had reverse-pitch propellers that permitted a short landing length and the facility to cruise under its own power. It was quite an experience to watch these large, seemingly ungainly machines land. They resembled a massive box, with a tailplane boom at the rear, and appeared to virtually drop from the sky. When the clamshell doors opened they revealed a cavernous interior that could hold small tanks, extremely large vehicles, and passengers in both the body of the aircraft and the boom. Some members of the squadron were obliged to travel, along with the equipment, in what appeared uncomfortable conditions. Watching these great lumbering beasts taking off was even more amusing as they trundled along the runway, seemingly unable to get off of the ground before lifting suddenly and climbing into the air almost vertically.

I did not relish the prospect of flying in one of those cumbersome beasts and my fears were allayed when a sparkling deHavilland Comet Mark 2 arrived to ferry the remainder of the airmen to Nicosia. The Comet was a premier aircraft of its day and it was a wonderful flight, the engines being virtually silent and vibration nil. I even stood a two shilling (10 pence) coin on its edge on a flat surface and it remained upright. The highlights of the fascinating views on offer were those overlooking the snow-crested Alps and the Bay of Naples. Such an experience would be commonplace today with the abundance of foreign holidays, but at that time it was a remarkable experience, unfortunately, not to be repeated.

We touched down in the midst of an extensive combined RAF and army camp outside Nicosia which covered several square miles, to be informed that security was tight and we would not be allowed off camp during our period of duty. Many British servicemen had been attacked or murdered in the unsettled political climate intensified by the desire for union with Greece (enosis), by the Greek Cypriots. A terrorist organization headed by Colonel Grivas, known as EOKA had opened a campaign against British rule in a well-coordinated series of attacks on police, military and other government installations in Nicosia, Famagusta, Larnaca and Limassol. Meanwhile a Turkish Resistance Organisation had been formed to fight EOKA and the island was on the verge of civil war. In response to the growing demand for enosis many Turkish Cypriots became convinced that their interests could only be protected by partition of the island into Greek and Turkish sectors. Events have shown that this was the eventual outcome.

Riding in trucks to our designated site we travelled on rough tracks through the surrounding scrubland. On our arrival the views beyond the perimeter fence were of mile after mile of desert only broken by the far-off vista of the Kyrenia Mountains to the north.

The camp occupants had swelled to many times larger than that before the unrest and much of the accommodation was under canvas, including ours. The weather was hot, but not uncomfortably so in October, but the food was disgusting and an abiding memory of my time at Nicosia is, as mentioned previously, of a meal of gristly meat balls floating in an excuse for gravy.

During the day our minds were occupied by work, for our Hunters were flying sorties for much of the time. The only

Hawker Hunters of 65 Squadron on standby at RAF Nicosia

relaxation during the evening was a visit to the NAAFI canteen on our site or to the Astra Cinema on camp. The NAAFI was not of the standard of those I had been used to, merely a large wooden-framed corrugated iron hut filled to the rafters with airmen and soldiers unsettlingly carrying weapons. I remember an incident when there was a loud bang in the vicinity of the hut and its occupants were galvanised into action. There were shouts of 'On the floor!' from soldiers who had experienced bomb attacks on the camp. The lights were slammed off and everyone dived onto the floor, to the sound of guns being cocked. Everything was silent for about ten minutes before the lights came on once more and everyone got up from the floor. It proved to be a false alarm, but a few nights later the hut was bombed by EOKA terrorists, or their sympathisers, which put paid to any socialising.

The sole remaining outlet for enjoyment was the cinema that I visited on one occasion. Despite there being a full house, the film was laughable, although it was not meant to be a comedy. It was supposedly a horror film in which monsters stalked the countryside. These beasts were pathetic; obviously models that

Off-duty at RAF Nicosia. The author is second from the right

moved jerkily and could not scare the skin off a rice pudding! These were the days before CGI's (Computer Generated Images).

It was very fortunate that no one was seriously injured when our NAAFI canteen was blown up. A few weeks later a bomb was planted in a NAAFI canteen on another site, with dire consequences. An airman was an eye witness to the explosion and described the event thus:

'I had a lucky escape. At around 9 pm the audience was leaving the nearby Astra Cinema and, along with other airmen I had been listening to the Everly Brothers' version of *All I Have to do is Dream* on the juke box in the NAAFI canteen and decided to leave by the side door. I had walked about twenty yards from the building when there was an almighty bang and I found myself flat on my face with my ears ringing. I picked myself up and could hear shouts from men running from all directions towards the canteen. As I turned I saw smoke and dust pouring from gaping holes in the corrugated iron structure. The bomb must have been placed by one of the four Greek Cypriots who worked in the canteen.

That evening they had tried to keep out of sight and we had complained about the poor service. The RAF lads were fed up with them not clearing the tables or serving the food we had ordered. We knew they disliked the British, particularly their manager, who hated our regular searches when Cypriots entered the camp each day.'

The explosion killed two airmen and severely wounded seven others. After the bombing of the NAAFI there was a rush to the armory with the intention of taking revenge in Nicosia. Everyone was incensed by the actions of the EOKA terrorists and if we had been allowed off camp there would have been a major incident. (British soldiers guarded servicemen's wives whilst they shopped in Nicosia).

When the head of the RAF in Cyprus heard the news of the bombing he immediately demanded the dismissal of all Greek Cypriot NAAFI employees. Next morning 4,000 of them were banned from entering any camp or NAAFI establishment on the island.

Following the exclusion of the Greek Cypriots, EOKA took revenge on two unfortunate British NAAFI officers whilst they inspected their butchery's cold store in Famagusta. Just as they were about to leave at the end of their working day, a gang of terrorists pushed them back inside the store, padlocked the door, switched off the lights and left. For the two men inside, wearing open neck shirts and light trousers, their chance of survival in a temperature of minus ten degrees Fahrenheit was nil. Fortunately, the prisoners found a large meat cleaver, with which they cut a hole in the wall of the cold store and were able to shout until someone heard their cries and rescued them.

Forty-six NAAFI canteens, seventeen shops, three clubs, two leave centres and several bakeries came to a standstill due to a shortage of Greek Cypriot staff. Temporarily, servicemen's and NAAFI staff's wives helped to maintain vital services and NAAFI Headquarters issued an S.O.S for 500 volunteers. Within twenty-four hours 17,000 people, mostly young women, volunteered, from all over Britain. Whatever their background they were filled with patriotism, a desire for adventure and a longing for the sun.

Sir Winston Churchill's Austrian cook was one of the

volunteers, apparently wishing to repay her debt to Britain. 'England gave me a home when I was homeless and starving,' she said, giving her reason for wishing to join the venture. She admitted to not informing Sir Winston and Lady Churchill of her request.

After the arrival of the first batch of NAAFI volunteers an eye witness remarked, 'The women's billets were surrounded by barbed wire and I never knew if it was to keep them in or to keep us out!'

The NAAFI bombings kept us all on our toes and extra guards were posted around the camp and the aircraft. Our spirits were kept up during our off-duty hours by listening to the radio and playing football.

At the weekend, a few days after our arrival, we were given some extra free time. There was a small market on camp with stalls managed by Cypriots which I visited, searching for souvenirs. There was no possibility of buying them elsewhere and I decided to risk involvement in another incident. There were plenty of goods on offer and the chance to indulge in some bartering, but all the time I was there I was looking out for signs of trouble. Were the Cypriot traders spies or terrorists I wondered? Fortunately the afternoon passed off peacefully.

On our seventh day at RAF Nicosia we were given some surprising news. The next day we were to leave for home. Our poor Flight Sergeants were bombarded with questions, such as, 'Why the sudden change of plan? Who was responsible for this foul-up?' We were told this was nothing to do with us and to just be glad to get out of Cyprus.

As it transpired, some of us, me included, nearly didn't. That evening we were instructed to pack our kit and take it to one of several trucks that were waiting to transfer it to the airport. The following morning everyone awoke early and waited excitedly to be off. Eventually, the trucks returned to ferry us to our aircraft around 8 am.

On the tarmac stood a beautiful, gleaming Comet waiting to take us back to England. We were told to wait in the airport building until instructed to board the plane. This was fortuitous, for whilst we were waiting, a small bomb exploded aboard the Comet damaging the fuselage. Apparently it had been

COMET SABOTAGE INQUIRY BEGUN

Cyprus Mail Reporter

The veil of mystery over the sabotage at Nicosia Airport lifted yesterday – but only slightly. An official spokesman said the Court of Enquiry had begun its operations headed by a senior RAF Officer.

The comet flew to El Adam Lybia late on Wednesday night – leaving all its 44 passengers behind.

Four of the ten injured were still in the British Military Hospital in Nicosia. Five others had been given medical treatment on the spot at the airport.

Yesterday security chiefs were tightening all airfield checks to seal the loopholes through which EOKA saboteurs have done devasting work.

The luggage which was waiting to be loaded on to the plane, when the bomb exploded in one bag, was not necessarily due to have been searched.

Wednesday's statement said the baggage would have been checked by security control, but it is understood this operation would not necessarily have meant a full search.

COMET NOT AT CIVIL AIRPORT

The Director of Civil Aviation wishes to emphasise that the sabotage incident to a Comet did not occur within the precincts of Nicosia Civil Airport.

*Cyprus Mail account
of Comet sabotage*

*The NAAFI at
RAF Nicosia
after the bomb
blast*

planted in our luggage and was obviously timed to be triggered in mid-air, with fatal consequences. Thankfully it exploded before we boarded the aircraft.

When we heard this news everyone went deathly quiet and no one spoke for some time. Eventually a Flight Lieutenant arrived to tell us that the Comet could not be used, a fact that we had already grasped, and we were to fly instead in a Handley Page Hastings. This aircraft, he explained had not the range of the Comet and we would be staying overnight in Malta.

This was good and bad news. We were still going home, albeit more slowly, but the two aircraft just did not compare and we would not be travelling in the same comfort we had enjoyed on our outward flight.

As the Hastings became airborne, I waved goodbye to Nicosia and Cyprus with the thought if I ever returned it would be, hopefully, in more peaceful conditions, for there had been no chance to explore the island. Unfortunately, I have not revisited Cyprus and the RAF terminated their involvement in RAF Nicosia in 1966, due to limited space caused by vastly increasing civilian aircraft movements. The airport closed in 1974, but it is still owned by the UK Ministry of Defence, and is controlled by the United Nations Peace-keeping Force in Cyprus and used by their helicopters for patrol purposes.

As a result of the Turkish invasion in 1974, Turkey occupied 37 percent of the island, splitting Cyprus into the Turkish North and the Greek South, which are served by different and more recently-opened airports.

Despite the Hastings being like an old 'banger' when compared to the first-rate Comet it had given faithful service to the RAF for ten years, as a long-range transport aircraft, flown by Transport Command. It was rushed into service because of the Berlin Airlift in September/October 1948, flying the first relief sorties in November of that year. The Hastings fleet was used mainly for carrying coal, of all things! In total around 55,000 tons of supplies were delivered until October 1949.

Hastings aircraft were also used during the Suez Crisis when they dropped paratroopers on El Gamil, a fortress with an airfield in Port Said Governorate, and they continued to provide transport support to British military operations around the world through the 1950's and 1960's. This included dropping supplies to troops in Malaysia during the Indonesian confrontation.

Our particular Hastings arrived safely in Valletta, the capital of the island of Malta and we were given the rest of the day and evening to look around the city, which was a real bonus. Flags displaying a George Cross were numerous and a reminder of Malta's accolade of being the 'George Cross Island.' The cross itself was awarded by King George VI in 1942 for the fortitude of its population under sustained air attacks and a naval blockade which almost starved it into submission. Italian and German bombers wrought havoc on the island and ammunition ran so low that anti-aircraft guns could only fire a few rounds each day.

As I and my companions walked the ancient streets of Valletta the ravages of World War Two were plain to see, for the conflict had ceased a mere thirteen years before our visit. On view were buildings dating from the sixteenth century onwards built during the rule of the Order of St. John, also known as the Knight's Hospitaller. Jean Parisot de la Vallette gave his name to the city in1565 when he defended the island from an Ottoman invasion. The city surrounds two natural harbours, Marsamxett and Grand Harbour, which lie side by side with their impressive fortifications built by the Knights. In fact, Valletta is a city that has suffered many raids and its numerous bastions and watch towers bear testament to this. One such incursion took place in 1798 when Napoleon Bonaparte took Valletta and stayed briefly at the Palazzo Parisio before continuing on his onslaught to Egypt.

Napoleon had been planning an invasion of Britain, but decided France's naval power was not strong enough to confront the Royal Navy in the English Channel. With this in mind he embarked on a military expedition to seize Egypt and thereby undermine Britain's access to its trade interest in India. His ultimate aim was to establish a French presence in the Middle East and form an alliance with a Muslim enemy of the British in India, Tipu Sultan. When Egypt had been captured his intention was to establish relations with the Indian princes and, together with them attack the overseas possessions of the British.

A Handley Page Hastings waiting to take us home

After leaving Valletta, Napoleon landed at Alexandria and was victorious in battle against the Mamluks, Egypt's ruling military caste. On 24th July 1798 he defeated the Egyptians at the Battle of the Pyramids, killing 2,000 of their number. He then suffered a grave setback on 1st August when the British fleet under Horatio Nelson captured or destroyed all but two French vessels during the Battle of the Nile, which frustrated Napoleon's goal of a strengthened position in the Mediterranean.

The Knights also built a seriesof impressive watchtowers at strategic locations around the city. Many of these still exist, together with sentry posts, across the city bastions. Amongst other highlights we paid a short visit to St. John's Co-Cathedral, which contains the only signed work and largest painting by Carravaggio, and gazed on the Magisterial Palace, now the seat of the Maltese Parliament.

Time did not permit a really close inspection of the impressive city that would have looked even more so without the attentions of the German and Italian bombers. Before continuing our homeward flight on the following morning there was an hour or two's opportunity to do more sight-seeing and I decided on a visit to Fort Saint Elmo. It lies on a peninsula that divides the two harbours and commands the entrances to both. The fort was the scene of the most intense fighting during the 1565 siege and it survived a stiff bombardment by Turkish cannon, during which a cannon shot from Fort St. Angelo across the Grand Harbour landed close to the Turkish battery. Debris from the impact mortally wounded the Ottoman admiral, ridding the defenders of one of the outstanding enemy leaders. However, in the long-term it did not prevent the overrunning of the fort by the Ottoman forces, although the siege had been withstood for over a month. The few Maltese defenders that survived did so by swimming across the Grand Harbour to Fort St. Angelo. Although the fort was reduced to rubble, it was rebuilt and strengthened when the Ottoman forces discontinued the siege of Valletta.

Today, the George Cross, awarded to the island, is on display in the National War Museum, which is housed in a section of the fort. Last year my wife and I were on a cruise of the Mediterranean and the Canary Islands. I was greatly anticipating visiting Valletta once more as it was on the ship's itinerary. Unfortunately I was unable to do this and to see how the city had changed over the intervening years, for the sea was too rough to allow our ship to enter the harbour. Sadly, a great opportunity was missed.

The Hastings with us aboard left Malta in the late morning, heading, as we thought, for Duxford airfield. However, it was a shock when the aircraft landed at RAF Waterbeach, a fighter base, lying six miles north of Cambridge and fourteen miles from Duxford. We soon learned the reason for this detour. The runway at Duxford had been partially dug up and was under repair! The plan had been, obviously, to carry out the repairs during our three-month stay in Cyprus, which had suddenly been shortened to a single week. I do not know who was responsible at the Air Ministry for this change of plan, but I was quite happy to be at Waterbeach, where there might be some decent food after the privation of Nicosia.

My hopes were justified as the omens looked favourable. Our meal that evening could not be faulted. The menu included around five choices for each course, which was magnificent. The Catering Officer must be well-respected, I reckoned, for actually spending the whole of his budget on food! Don't hurry with the runway repairs was the general feeling!

Everyone was in good spirits that evening after hearing that we had been given one week's leave and would be based at Waterbeach for five weeks. It was good to sleep in a normal RAF bed again and to savour the thought of a splendid breakfast on the following morning.

Again I was not disappointed. The breakfast was second to none, just the thing for setting me up for a hitch-hike to my home in Mansfield. This was my normal means of travel to and from Duxford, much of the journey being along the A1, which at that time was well below the present standard. It wound through each town en route before the days of by-passes. Stamford, Grantham and Newark that I passed through were clogged with traffic. Large lorries knocked lumps of masonry from buildings situated on tight corners, particularly in the lovely old town of Stamford. It was once a major mill town and it still retains its old-world charm. Many of its buildings are constructed from Lincolnshire limestone, which add to its attraction.

Anyone who has hitch-hiked will know that waiting for a lift is an uncertain activity. Despite accepting a ride in any kind of vehicle my waiting time varied from ten minutes to two hours. I was given a lift by a lorry driver one evening in a chugging old vehicle who seemed surprised at my acceptance of a lift. 'I'm not used to 'Brylcream Boys' (a reference to the RAF being, supposedly, a cut above the rest of the forces), travelling with me. I thought you lads only travelled in cars,' he said. I explained about not being concerned only with comfortable vehicles, which he thought was commendable.

I got to know the best places to wait by the roadside for a lift and also to know driver's stopping places. I would often have a snack with drivers at cafés, whilst they enjoyed a break and a meal. In fact, I could have written a guide book to the best transport cafés in five counties. An outstanding one was situated on a hilltop just outside Grantham, Margaret Thatcher's home town, although she had not come to the fore back then.

I had several memorable experiences whilst hitch-hiking, including the time when I had been squeezed in between two people travelling in the back seat of a car for some time. When they let me out I could not stand up, my legs having gone dead. I leant on the boot of the car for support and slowly slid to the ground. The looks on the faces of the car's occupants signified they thought I was drunk!

On another occasion, when strictly I was not hitch-hiking, but was being given a lift in the car of a Flight Sergeant, who was also stationed at RAF Duxford, an alarming discovery was made. We were speeding along the road towards Huntingdon when a worrying knocking sound developed and steering became difficult. Thankfully, the Flight Sergeant pulled into the roadside to investigate and found the four nuts securing one of the front wheels were on virtually the last thread of the bolts. He remedied this quickly, explaining he had changed the wheel the previous evening and forgotten to tighten the nuts.

To return to my journey back home from Waterbeach, I had decided not to tell my family of the change of schedule and it came as a great surprise to them when I appeared on the doorstep. My father had served in the RAF during the Second World War and declared that you could be shunted around at a moment's notice and you just had to accept the fact. I told him I did not mind accepting my latest move as it was quite fortuitous.

Returning to camp after my leave I spent five pleasant weeks before returning to Duxford, but RAF Waterbeach appeared to have a jinx on some members of the squadron. One member, nicknamed 'Ginger Pig,' and built like a brick outhouse, fell from a first floor window. Luckily, he survived with cuts and bruises, probably because of all the 'padding' on his chubby frame. Another unfortunate incident befell one of my friends, which makes my eyes water at the thought of it. He trapped a vital part of his anatomy in his trouser zip and drew blood, which meant a visit to the sick bay. On his return he said it had been a most painful experience when he was finally released from his predicament. Fortunately, he had been attended to by a medical orderly and not a nurse.

Both these unfortunates received merciless ribbing, all part

Ground crew preparing a Hawker Hunter of 65 Squadron for flight

of the banter that was a normal part of squadron life. If you came from 'up north', as the cockneys put it, they would imitate a broad Yorkshire accent when talking to you. We 'northeners' chided the London upstarts and described them as 'all mouth and no trousers.' They believed that everyone living north of Watford was a savage, or wore a flat cap, to which we would reply, 'Eh by gum, it's better than being a pansy.'

On one occasion the banter had become sickening. There was always antagonism between the airmen over their support for their preferred football team. Manchester and Lancashire lads usually supported Manchester United, Manchester City, or Liverpool and the cockneys followed London clubs, such as Arsenal, or Tottenham Hotspur. The Manchester United supporters amongst us were always bragging about their brilliant team and the 'Busby Babes,' as they were known. Under their manager, Matt Busby, the team had become very successful and included many talented young players, such as Duncan Edwards, Dennis Viollet and Tommy Taylor.

The previous February it had been announced over the radio that seven Manchester United footballers were among twenty-one people killed in an air crash at Munich airport. Apparently, the plane was bringing the team and other personnel, including sports journalists, from a European Cup match against Red Star Belgrade, in Yugoslavia, and had landed at the airport to refuel. Weather conditions were treacherous when the plane prepared to take off and two abortive attempts were made. On the third attempt the aircraft overshot the runway, due to slush lying on it, hit two buildings and burst into flames. Remarkably, the fuselage did not catch fire and some of those who had escaped serious injury went back into the wreckage to rescue those still in there.

After the radio announcement the cockneys were crowing as though they had scored some points over their northern antagonists. I felt that a bit of banter was okay but was unhappy with the attitude of the Londoners. How could anyone be unaffected by the demise of young Manchester United players, such as Roger Byrne, Eddie Colman, Tommy Taylor and Duncan Edwards? The team had been decimated in one cruel twist of fate and one would expect football supporters everywhere to unite in sympathy. Perhaps the boasting of the lads supporting Manchester United had really got to them.

There was, however, some consolation for the ravaged team's supporters. Among the survivors was the manager, Matt Busby, as he was then, also Bobby Charlton who became probably the club's greatest ever striker. They and several other players who survived helped to revive the fortunes of the iconic football club. Even by the time the season was over in May the team had reached the F.A. Cup Final, only to be beaten by Bolton Wanderers.

On returning to Duxford, life resumed as normal and I got my old bed back. The familiar pattern of aircraft inspection and minor repairs kept me occupied and I struggled to catch up with my college studies, having missed six weeks of the course through my trip to Cyprus and the spell at Waterbeach. Possibly due to the break in my studies I narrowly failed my exams the following May, missing out by three marks in one of the subjects.

I also began to go to rugby training once more, hoping to get into the station team. Despite being a reserve on several occasions I was unable to do so. The majority of the players were officers and this may have had some bearing on my non-selection.

Most Friday afternoons saw me making for the A1 and Mansfield. It was a nice feeling to arrive home in the late evening and look forward to a weekend out of uniform. I remember vividly the programme that was often being broadcast on television (in black and white) when I entered the house. It was *The Army Game*, a sitcom about a group of National Servicemen. I could not escape conscription, even at home! It concerned the antics of a squad of wayward soldiers and their overbearing Sergeant Major. Does this seem familiar? Shades of square-bashing at Bridgnorth!

Several of the programme's stars became household names during the next three decades, including Bill Fraser and Alfie Bass, who appeared later in a spin-off from that series entitled *Bootsy and Snudge*, with Bill Fraser as the Sergeant Major and Alfie Bass as the down-trodden private. *The Army Game* ran for five series and 154 episodes and a group of the actors performed a short scene from it at the Royal Variety Performance attended by Queen Elizabeth the Queen Mother in 1959. This was the last Royal Variety Performance not to be televised. Some of *The Army Game's* stars appeared subsequently in the *Carry On* films, such as Bernard Bresslaw, Charles Hawtrey and Dick Emery.

Bernard Bresslaw, who had appeared as the gormless Private Popplewell in *The Army Game,* had a song entitled *Mad Passionate Love* reach number five in the UK singles chart. Dick Emery became a well-known comedian, appearing in a string of his own television series. In some of his sketches he dressed in drag and became known for his catchphrase, 'Oh, you are awful!'

Listening to an hour of 'Rock and Roll' numbers on the car radio recently took me back to Duxford 1958 when the craze was at its height. This unique sound arrived like a bolt from the blue from America and revolutionised the popular music scene in Britain. The singular tones of Buddy Holly, tragically killed in an air crash, transported me to those heady days when teenagers were captivated by the new and bewitching beat and were even lured into rebellion by Bill Haley and the Comets. During the band's performances, particularly the number *Rock around the Clock,* in theatres and cinemas, the young audiences began dancing in the aisles and ripping up seats, much to the horror of the establishments' managers and the public. In mitigation, people had never heard such tantalising and vibrant music and there was plenty of it provided by the likes of Fats Domino, Little Richard, Conway Twitty (who on earth came up with that name?) Eddie Cochran . . . the list is endless.

The principal pioneer of Rock and Roll was Buddy Holly, whose success lasted, sadly, a mere year and a half. He was described by one music critic as 'the single most influential creative force in early Rock and Roll.' His demise took place in the early hours of 3 February 1959 when he had chartered a small airplane to take him to the next stage of a three-week tour of the American Midwest. This came about due to the bitterly cold weather and the fact that the coach, in which he and his band were touring, was plagued with a faulty heating system. Tragically, the aircraft crashed soon after take-off, cutting short the life of a remarkably talented musician.

Whilst I was stationed at Duxford I encountered three outstanding officers. Two Station Commanders: Group Captain Herbert Moreton Pinfold and Group Captain Norman Ryder who followed him, and Squadron Leader Charles Maughan, who eventually rose to the rank of Air Marshall.

The two Group Captains were veterans of the Battle of Britain, Pinfold flying Hurricanes and Ryder flying Spitfires at that crucial period of the Second World War. Herbert Pinfold returned from service with the RAF overseas in 1936 and joined the newly-formed 64 Squadron, equipped with Hawker Demons. After a posting to the western desert he qualified as a flying instructor and operated in this capacity at several postings until August 1940 when he took command of 56 Squadron at North Weald, a matter of days after the beginning of the Battle of Britain. Here he flew Hurricanes, having just converted to them. He was thrown in at the deep end, the squadron having suffered continual casualties and both previous Flight Commanders had been shot down just before his arrival. His first five days as Squadron Leader were hectic. He flew fourteen sorties, three in one day, with only eight available operational pilots. After a week of action the squadron was so depleted he had to take in pilots from Poland and Czechoslovakia.

It was said that the relentless pressure, at the height of the Battle of Britain in September 1940, weighed so heavily on RAF pilots, who, starved of sleep, could experience lapses of concentration. One such pilot recalled, 'you could be airborne and climbing at a thousand feet above the airfield wondering how you had got there, your mind a complete blank. Fatigue could cause you to doze-off inadvertently for a few seconds or minutes, which was quite terrifying.'

On the 30th September Pinfold's squadron was scrambled to intercept a large formation of enemy bombers over Portland. The bombers had fighter support and were heading for a strategic aircraft factory at Yeovil in Somerset. With just six Hurricanes for support Pinfold attacked, not head-on, but from the side, giving his pilots a greater chance of damaging the bombers with long bursts of machine gun fire. Within seconds a frantic dog-fight developed, during which Pinfold shot down a Dornier, but his aircraft was hit by return fire. The cooling tank in his Hurricane exploded and the cockpit filled with fumes. Visibility was almost nil, but he succeeded in nursing his aircraft down safely. Later, he learned that the bombing raid had been a disaster for the Germans. Due to thick cloud they had dropped their bombs on Sherborne by mistake, causing considerable loss of civilian life.

An incident, in October 1940, involving Pinfold demonstrates the lighter side of Squadron life during those hectic and dangerous days. He was due for an annual medical inspection at the RAF Hospital, Halton. His adjutant offered to take him by car for the appointment. It was arranged that during this excursion an attempt would be made to obtain a long overdue squadron mascot, the majority of the squadron being in favour of a dog. Prior to the journey a considerable amount of alcoholic refreshment was consumed resulting in the pair returning with a monkey. The pilots immediately named it 109 and told any visiting dignitaries that the animal was being trained to sit behind the pilots, facing backwards. When airborne, the monkey would look out for German fighters

Wing Commander (later Group Captain)
Herbert Moreton Pinfold
(By kind permission of the H.M. Pinfold Collection)

Flight Lieutenant (later Group Captain) Norman Ryder with
fellow pilots of 41 Squadron at Hornchurch in 1941.
He is second from the right

(Me 109's) on their tail and tap the pilot on the shoulder
when one was sited. It is not known what the dignitaries
thought of this outrageous tale, but the monkey never got
airborne and it went absent without leave one day when it
disappeared into the woods near dispersal!

Pinfold survived the Battle of Britain and by the end of the
year he was leading his squadron on daily patrols over France.
During 1940, 56 Squadron claimed over 100 enemy aircraft
shot down. At the end of January 1941, Herbert Pinfold
returned to flying training, having done his bit in fighting off
the Luftwaffe. Later he completed the RAF Staff College course
and was deployed in a number of staff positions in the UK and
overseas. Following these he took command of RAF Duxford
that was at that time equipped with Meteors. After a break, when
he was posted to the Air Ministry and later appointed Air Attache
in Rome, Herbert returned to Duxford in 1956 for a second spell
in charge of the station. On the 1st of October 1958 he retired
from the RAF, I having known him for a mere few

months. However, I shall also remember him as a fair and courteous man who took the time to chat with airframe mechanics as they strapped him into the cockpit before a flight.

Norman Ryder, who replaced Herbert Pinfold, was a fighter ace, with eight recorded kills. He was a school teacher before the Second World War and he became the first RAF pilot to ditch a Spitfire in April 1940, after shooting down a German Heinkel. He was a Flight Lieutenant with 41 Squadron at RAF Hornchurch in 1941, establishing himself as a first-class fighter pilot. Promotion was quick in those uncertain times and later that year he reached the rank of Wing Commander. Whilst leading the Kenly Wing escorting Hurricanes to Dunkirk he was shot down by flak. His plane crashed on the beach and the wrecked Spitfire, known as the 'Kiwi Spitfire' having been purchased by the Spitfire Fund donations of New Zealanders, was photographed later by a German. Norman Ryder was taken prisoner but survived the war.

I recall one day at Duxford standing in formation near the hangars and seeing him with Douglas Bader a short distance away. This was quite an event for me, being close to two such eminent ex-fighter pilots. I wish they had come over to where our Squadron Leader was addressing the men. Unfortunately, I had no close contact with either of them, but I was reminded of that day some years later whilst watching the 1969 film *The Battle of Britain*, for one scene, involving Kenneth More and Susannah York was shot in that very spot.

Squadron Leader Charles Maughan, who had a different pedigree to Ryder, but an equally impressive one, assumed command of 65 Squadron in 1958. He had served in the Second World War as a pilot in the Fleet Air Arm, flying biplane 'Stringbag' Swordfish anti-submarine patrol bombers before piloting the Supermarine Seafire fighters, the naval version of the Spitfire. During the latter period he flew sorties from escort carriers on convoys from Londonderry to Halifax, Nova Scotia. He left the Fleet Air Arm in 1946 and worked for a time with the GPO. However, he yearned to fly once more and in 1949 he enlisted in the RAF and his first operational posting was to 263 Squadron, which flew Meteors. Then he saw service with Vampire and Venom squadrons in the UK and Germany.

By 1959 he had made 65 Squadron a very efficient unit. Probably the most conspicuous feat of his command was making headlines in the National Press in July 1959 by winning the Daily Mail London to Paris Air Race that was held to celebrate the fiftieth anniversary of Louis Bleriot's pioneering cross-channel flight. It became known as the 'Arch to Arc' contest, which began at Marble Arch and ended at the Arc de Triomphe and involved the competitors in some desperate situations, not merely in the air but on the roads of the two capital cities.

The rules of the race stipulated that the laws and regulations of each country were observed and the race was open to anyone, using any form of transport they chose. More than 200 competitors entered, ranging from well-organised teams, such as those of the RAF, to eccentric individuals.

Initially, Group Captain Ryder, Charles and his squadron thought it merely 'a good idea to enter,' but this soon grew into a major operation involving all sections of the Duxford contingent. In order to be within reach of Central London, the race's starting point, the race team of RAF personnel deployed to RAF Biggin Hill along with the twin-seater Hunter to be used in the race. After numerous practice runs the operation was refined to a high degree.

During practice for the race Maughan arranged (illegally) for the traffic lights on the route from Marble Arch to Chelsea to be held on green by getting his airmen from 65 Squadron to jump up and down on the pressure pads in the road. Unfortunately, the police got wise to this scheme and put a stop to it.

Detailed accounts of Maughan's exploits in the race have been recorded and were featured in the Press at the time. He was driven at a furious pace as pillion passenger on a motor cycle from Marble Arch to Chelsea Embankment, where a helicopter was waiting to transfer him to Biggin Hill. On his arrival there he immediately climbed into the twin-seater Hunter, piloted by Flight Lieutenant Jim Burns and sped over the Channel to touch down at an air base south of Paris. Another helicopter was waiting there to ferry him to the centre of Paris and to allow him to board another motor cycle to get him as close to the Arc de Triomphe as it could, within France's highway regulations. The Squadron Leader then completed the course with a hundred-yard dash to the finishing line.

On the last of his several runs over the course, (competitors were allowed to make a number of attempts over the two-week period allotted to the race) he achieved the remarkable winning time of forty minutes and forty-four seconds. He was awarded the Air Force Cross for his feat. The leader of the RAF team, Group Captain Ryder, came third in a time of forty-two minutes and six seconds, having injured his leg in a motor cycle incident in Paris. In second place was a civilian, Eric Rylands, Managing Director of Skyways, in 41 minutes and forty-one seconds. Prizes were awarded to the first three finishers in the race. Maughan received £5,000, Rylands £2,500 and Ryder £1,500. There was an additional prize for the most original and commendable effort, which was awarded to the 'Bealine Syndicate,' a group of BEA executives and colleagues, who completed the course by bus, train, Comet aircraft and taxi in just over one hour. I found these completion times astounding, particularly that of the BEA entrants.

Talking of skill and achievement casts my mind back to another praiseworthy feat by a pilot of 65 Squadron. I was privileged to watch this Flight Lieutenant's action of landing his crippled Hunter on the Duxford runway. The plane had returned to base with an undercarriage problem – one of the main wheels remained stubbornly retracted and the pilot circled the airfield as the fire and rescue crew assembled at the end of the runway. He touched down on his one good main wheel and nose wheel and remained perfectly level and stable as the aircraft ran along the runway. The pilot was able to eventually slow it right down and veer onto the grass before coming to a halt. There was no fire or major damage to the plane and the pilot calmly waited for the rescue team to bring a ladder, which he climbed down and gave anyone in earshot a blasting about faulty workmanship.

By contrast, on an almost identical occasion, another pilot landed with one main wheel jammed in the up position. Instead of gliding down the runway, as the other pilot had done the plane keeled over to one side with the wing scraping on the tarmac sending up showers of sparks. The pilot managed to get the plane upright once more before it keeled over again and the process was repeated along nearly the length of the runway. For the last twenty yards or so, with the wing scraping the tarmac it shuddered to a grinding halt. Smoke began to pour from the damaged wing and the rescue team was quick to spray it with foam whilst the pilot was released from the cockpit. Having witnessed both incidents I was amazed at the contrast in ability between the two pilots.

I was reminded of Duxford's runway in 1986 whilst walking the Pennine Way. I had started fell-walking six years previously and this 270-mile trek was my first long-distance walk. A section of the Way passes through the Yorkshire Dales, an area I have come to know very well, and I stayed overnight at the Youth Hostel in the popular Dales village of Malham on my journey. That evening there were only four people in the hostel, myself, a young man I had met some days previously and a married couple named Ian and Sheila, who were walking part of the Way. I discovered that they lived close to the end of the runway at Duxford and that Ian, although of slim build, could eat like a horse.

The warden placed a large pan of soup before us at dinner. When we had all consumed at least four helpings the warden told us to eat up or the remains would go to waste. Everyone laughingly agreed that this was too much of a good thing, except Ian that is, who said he would happily finish the remaining contents. To our amazement, not only did he polish off every last drop, he even scraped out the pan and the dregs from the ladle! He appeared to have no problem eating the rest of the meal.

Afterwards Ian produced his party piece, in the form of a tea bag. He claimed to hold the world record for the number of cups of tea from one bag – sixteen! I kept company with Ian and Sheila for much of the remainder of the walk and I was able to witness his remarkable prowess, as he performed the teabag routine each evening. I'm glad that I never had to sample the tea that he produced after the third cup as there was very little colour to it by the fourteenth!

During my time at Duxford I became friends with a fellow airframe mechanic on 65 Squadron, who lived in nearby

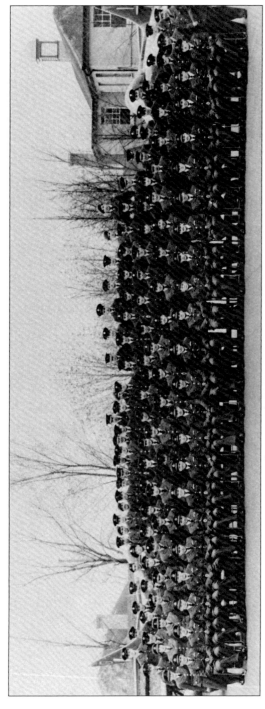

65 Squadron at RAF Duxford in 1959

Pilots and ground crew of 64 and 65 Squadrons with their aircraft at RAF Duxford. 65 Squadron is on the right of the photograph.

Cambridge. I have very pleasant memories of evenings spent with Brian and his wife Margaret, who provided me with supper of soup and 'soldiers' (pieces of toast cut into strips). I was very grateful for their hospitality and the opportunity to spend evenings away from camp. After demob, my wife and I paid two enjoyable visits to their new home in Basildon. Recently, I met my old colleague Brian, after an interval of forty-five years, to reminisce about our time at Duxford. He kindly helped me to fill in some of the gaps in my memory regarding the station and he related some of his experiences to include in this book.

One of these concerned the accident involving the inadvertent firing of the drogue gun in the Hawker Hunter that I mentioned previously. He revealed that he actually witnessed the incident, which came as a surprise to me. Apparently, Brian, who was also an airframe mechanic, was checking round the aircraft when the drogue gun activated.

A humorous incident that Brian recalled involved a collision between a Landrover and a stationary Hunter. It was caused by carelessness on the part of the Senior Technician driving the vehicle. He was either driving too fast or was inattentive and he struck the wing of one of the Hunters lined up at dispersal, damaging the aileron (the hinged portion of an aircraft's wing used to control the roll of the aircraft about its longitudinal axis). Mortified by what he had done the Senior Technician sprang into action and with the help of the ground crew he removed the damaged aileron and hid it in a hangar. Then he procured a new one and rapidly replaced the old one. Mercifully, this episode passed unnoticed by anyone in authority, which was lucky because he could have been severely reprimanded or even court-marshalled.

I asked Brian why he had not flown to Cyprus with the rest of the squadron in 1958 and he told me that Margaret was expecting a baby and he was allowed to remain at Duxford on compassionate grounds. He also informed me that his place was taken by Brian Bedford, another member of the squadron who I instantly remembered because we were demobbed on the same day and agreed to send a telegram to each other to be read out at our respective wedding receptions. I sent a telegram on the appointed day saying, 'Hope this finds you as it leaves me;

married!' Unfortunately I did not receive one in return.

Many veterans keep in contact through the Old Dux Association, which unites friends who have lost touch over the years. It also provides an opportunity to recapture the spirit, and experience the uniqueness of, RAF Duxford. It is said that at Old Dux get-togethers there is still a friendly rivalry between former members of 64 and 65 squadrons!

I came to know Cambridge very well during my time at the station and re-visited the city during my recent trip to Duxford. I found it to be still a very vibrant and attractive city. The only drawback is that you must be wary of the multitude of bicycles that throng the streets, some of them quite narrow, but it is a compact city, easy to get around.

Its ancient buildings are delightful, particularly the colleges, although I only viewed the courtyard of many of them through their gateways. The highlight is probably Kings College Chapel as seen from The Backs. This imposing Gothic building was constructed during the latter period of the fifteenth century and the early part of the sixteenth century, in fact it took just over one hundred years. Henry VI, founder of two great colleges, King's and Eton, was only nineteen years old when he laid the first stone in 1441. Although still a young man Henry was determined that the Chapel would be unequalled in size and beauty. The foundation stone was laid in 1446 by Henry as part of his grand plan for a great court, of which the Chapel was to form the north side, but, unfortunately, the scheme was never realised and only the Chapel was completed.

In 1455 the Wars of the Roses broke out and Edward, Duke of York, later Edward IV, challenged Henry's right to the throne, but for the first eleven years building continued under Henry's patronage. The construction of the Chapel and the Wars of the Roses were closely linked and in 1461 Henry was taken prisoner by Edward and was murdered in the Tower of London ten years later. Very little building of the Chapel then took place until Edward's death in 1483.

Richard III, who succeeded Edward, ordered work to be resumed and considerable progress was made. However, it was Henry VII and Henry VIII who completed the magnificent edifice. After its completion the Chapel was recognized as one of Europe's greatest medieval buildings.

King's College Chapel emerged unscathed from the Second World War when the fine medieval glass from most of the windows was removed for safety, only the West Window remaining in place.

Another source of the city's charm is its lovely stretches of rolling lawns and colourful gardens, threaded by the winding River Cam lined with boathouses and spanned by historic, shapely bridges. From the bridges I could watch the progress of oarsmen and women straining every sinew in their sleek craft as they passed beneath and also the more sedate punts making steady progress through The Backs. Maliciously, I used to wish for the sight of a 'gondolier' getting his pole stuck in the riverbed and clinging to it as the punt drifted away from him. My ungentlemanly wish was never realised.

In November 1958, I entered the last six months of my service with excitement rising to a crescendo as the months passed. However, that was nothing compared to the airmen who kept a chart of each day of their service and crossed one off each evening. Just imagine the thrill of a National Serviceman eliminating the first day's record and declaring, 'Only another 729 days to do!'

Just before the great day of my demob I was interviewed by an officer who tried to persuade me to 'sign on' for a regular term. I explained that I had enjoyed my two years but I had no inclination to make a career of the RAF. It must have been put quite forcibly, for he answered, 'I can see that there is no point in trying to change your mind.'

Finally, the great day arrived and I was able to don my 'civvies' and walk out of the camp gate to freedom, waving a cheery goodbye to Duxford and the RAF.

Of course, 'absence makes the heart grow fonder' and memories surface and grow as the years pass and you remember the good times and wonder, 'what has happened to various old comrades?' Whilst searching through my old photographs for inclusion in this book I came across the signatures of my fellow RAF Bridgnorth 'sufferers' of Hut 22 on the reverse of one of them, which made up for the agonies we shared during square-bashing.

ROYAL AIR FORCE

R.A.F. FORM 1394.
(Revised December, 1951.)
(For issue only to National
Service Airmen and Airwomen
not on regular engagements).

BRIEF STATEMENT OF SERVICE AND CERTIFICATE ON DISCHARGE

1. Surname ......Plowright...................... Official No....5045445........
   Christian Names ...Alan................ Rank on Discharge ...S.A.C.
2. Period of whole-time service. From ...27th May, 1957............. To ...26th May, 1959.
3. Trade in civil life.......................... 4. R.A.F. trade on entry..Acr. asst. u/t Afr. mech.
5. Details of any R.A.F. trade training ..Trained at 10 S of T.T. on the A/fr. mech. (L/P)
   course, from 21st August, 1957 to 25th November, 1957 - Result - PASS
6. R.A.F. trade on discharge and brief description of duties. (vide A.M. Pamphlet 51.)
   Undertakes routine servicing of landplane airframes and their accessories,
   systems, components, and controls, undertakes functional checking of
   hydraulically, electrically, and pneumatically controlled and operated
   airframe components. Charges oleo legs with oil and air. Adjusts brakes.
7. Assessments of Conduct, Proficiency and Personal Qualities during service :—

	Exemplary	Very Good	Good	Fairly Good	Poor
(a) Conduct	X				
	Exceptional	Very Good	Good	Fairly Good	Poor
(b) Ability as tradesman/~~supervisor~~			X		
(c) Ability as supervisor in his trade					
(d) Personal Qualities :—					
(i) Leadership				X	
(ii) Co-operation			X		

*Delete as inapplicable
(Applicable to N.C.O.s only)
(iii) Bearing (to be assessed "Very Smart," "Smart," or "Untidy") Smart

8. Medals, Clasps, Decorations,
   Mentions in Despatches, etc........Nil
9. Reason for Discharge ..."On completion of whole time service"
10. REMARKS. (This section to be used only to amplify Assessments, trade qualifications, etc., where necessary.)
    He has been employed on first line servicing of Hunter aircraft, and
    has proved a reliable worker at all times.

11. DESCRIPTION ON DISCHARGE
    Height...5....ft...10...ins.   Colour of Hair ......Auburn
    Complexion ...Pale   Marks or Scars App. scar, scar side
    Colour of Eyes .Light blue   of left eye.
12. National Service airmen are liable to undergo part-time service—See notice overleaf.

UNIT DATE STAMP
2 6 MAY 1959

Signed .... Rank Flt. Off.
For Officer Commanding ....Royal Air Force Duxford

Signature of Airman/~~Airwoman~~ ...A. Plowright

(*3905—1203) Wt. 38040—3063 3,600 Pads 3/52 T.S. 839

Certificate received at the end of my two-year service

CHAPTER SEVEN

History of RAF Duxford, including the Battle of Britain and Sir Douglas Bader

Duxford airfield was built during the First World War, becoming one of the earliest RAF stations. In 1917 the Royal Flying Corps (RFC) expanded and Duxford was one of several new stations established to train RFC aircrew. At the beginning of April 1918 the Royal Naval Air Service and the Royal Flying Corps were merged to form the Royal Air Force. In September of that year Duxford opened as a flying school and, after the war ended, it was used as a base for the disbandment of squadrons from the Continent.

RAF Duxford became No. 2 Flying Training School in 1920, equipped with Avro 504's and the Bristol Fighter. In 1923 a training flight of Sopwith Snipes was added to the School and the following year Duxford became a fighter station.

By the beginning of 1925 Duxford's three fighter squadrons were up to strength with Gloster Grebes and Armstrong Whitworth Siskins. 19 Squadron was re-equipped with Bristol Bulldogs in 1931 and in 1935 was picked as the first squadron to fly the RAF's fastest new fighter, the Gloster Gauntlet. This aircraft attained speeds of up to 230 mph and the squadron gained an enviable reputation for formation flying and air-firing. Consequently, 19 Squadron was chosen to give a special demonstration of air drill over Duxford in 1935 on the occasion of King George V's Jubilee Review of the Royal Air Force.

In 1936 Flight Lieutenant Frank Whittle, later to be knighted and attain the rank of Air Commodore, was studying at Cambridge University and flew regularly from Duxford as a member of the Cambridge University Air Squadron. He was the first person to develop the jet turbine as a means of powering aircraft and his engineering genius enabled Britain to design the jet-powered Gloster Meteor in 1943.

Duxford was the first aerodrome in Fighter Command to be equipped with the new Supermarine Spitfires in the summer of 1938 such was its reputation at that time. The first of these aircraft was delivered to Duxford by no less than Jeffrey Quill,

Supermarine's chief test pilot. The Gauntlet was outdated by this time, but it was with this aircraft that 19 and 66 Squadrons stood at readiness during the Munich crisis of that year. It was following his meeting with Adolf Hitler that the Prime Minister, Neville Chamberlain, returned with the document signed by Hitler and gave rise to the famous phrase, 'Peace in our time.'

The station became even more prominent during the early part of the Second World War as part of 12 Group defending the industrial Midlands and north-east England during the Battle of Britain. At this time there was a great difference of opinion regarding tactics within Fighter Command and a controversy surrounded Duxford through the 'Big Wing' theories and experimentation involving Douglas Bader and Trafford Leigh-Mallory during the Battle of Britain.

Bader joined the RAF in 1928 after winning one of six annual prize cadetships offered by the RAF College at Cranwell each year. Here he excelled at sports, adding hockey and boxing to his list. Bader proved a headstrong and daring cadet who indulged in banned activities such as speeding, pillion-racing and racing motor cars, which nearly resulted in his expulsion.

On the 13th of September 1928 Bader had his first flight with an instructor and after a mere eleven hours and 15 minutes of flight time he flew solo for the first time. He competed for the 'Sword of Honour' award at the end of his two-year course, but was beaten by his nearest rival, Patrick Coote, who went on to become a Wing Commander before his death whilst flying as an observer in a Bristol Blenheim in 1941.

Bader was commissioned as a Pilot Officer in 1930, flying with 23 Squadron in Gloster Gamecocks and later, Bristol Bulldogs. Always a daredevil he often performed illegal and dangerous stunts. Despite strict instructions forbidding unauthorised aerobatics below 2,000 feet and to keep above 500 feet, Douglas frequently ignored what he took to be an unnecessary safety rule. Unfortunately, this proved his undoing when he indulged in some low-flying aerobatics at Woodley airfield, apparently prompted by a dare. During a dangerous roll manoeuvre one of the aircraft's wing-tips touched the ground causing a horrific crash. Bader was rushed to a nearby hospital, where both his legs were amputated – one above and one below the knee. He nearly died, but recovered after a long convalescence and was fitted with a pair of artificial legs. After an agonising period of trying to walk with his new and chafing legs, his persistence paid off and he was able to walk unaided.

Fighting hard to regain his former prowess – he had achieved the accolade of performing in and winning the Hendon Airshow 'pairs' event in 1931 before his accident – Douglas was able to drive a specially adapted motor car, play golf and even dance.

When he had fully recovered, it was necessary to prove to the RAF that he could still fly and that he was physically fit. It was arranged for him to have a trial in an Avro 504 which he was able to fly without a problem and a subsequent medical examination proved him to be fit for active service. In April 1933, this decision was tragically reversed on the grounds that his situation was not covered by King's Regulations. He was offered a ground occupation, which he grudgingly accepted and was posted to RAF Duxford, where he took over the transport section. Life became irksome although the job was easy and involved drinking gallons of tea, signing chits and giving orders concerning vehicles. The worst part was watching the pilots, some of whom he knew, enjoying their flying. Eventually, he was put out of his misery by an instruction from the Air Ministry that he could no longer be employed in the General Duties branch of the RAF. Shortly afterwards Bader was invalided out of the service and reduced to working in the office of an oil company. Nevertheless, he married Thelma Edwards, who he had come to know whilst convalescing and he had a small RAF pension in addition to his salary.

During the anxious period just before the outbreak of the Second World War Douglas pestered the Air Ministry to allow him to join the RAF once more and to go on active service and fly again. Eventually, he was asked to attend a selection board meeting, which proved to be of no assistance to his strenuous efforts to return to flying. He was informed that only 'ground' positions were on offer. Luckily for him, Air Vice Marshal Halahan, commandant of RAF Cranwell when Bader was a cadet there recommended him for assessment by the Central Flying School and, in October 1939, Douglas underwent a refresher course there. Initially reluctant to grant him flying

Duxford Aerodrome shortly after its construction in 1918

category status, the RAF granted his wish to resume operational flying.

Bader returned to Central Flying School at Upavon for a refresher course on current aircraft and eight years after his crash he flew solo once more in an Avro Tutor. Exhilarated, he could not resist turning the aircraft upside down and flying over the airfield at an altitude of 600 feet, managing to escape the wrath of any onlookers. He progressed to flying the Fairey Battle and Miles Master. The Battle, a single-engined, two-seater bomber was approaching the end of its useful life. Despite its drawback, Douglas mastered the modern gadgets it contained and avoided the classic mistakes of landing with the undercarriage up or attempting to take off with the propeller in course pitch. Upavon had a single Hurricane and Spitfire and Bader was extremely anxious to fly them, but had to wait in a long queue before being allowed to fly the former.

At that time he, like many others, did not pay much heed to the war (this was the period known as the 'Phoney War') and the approaching winter called a temporary truce in the fighting in Europe. One incident at this time introduced a little amusement. He received a letter marked 'secret' in large red type that informed him a great state of emergency had arisen and in view of this he had been posted to Upavon some weeks previously and a rail warrant was enclosed. The RAF could be relied on to produce these little blunders!

In early 1940 Bader returned to Duxford in a happier frame of mind than on his first visit and he joined 19 Squadron as its oldest pilot. By this time the squadron's reputation was such that it had become the first to re-equip with the Spitfire and Douglas got his chance to fly one at last. The aircraft started easily and he took off eagerly, soon feeling in tune with the splendid machine.

For the next three months Bader took part in formation-flying practice, tactics and convoy patrol. His first flight over a convoy proved an anti-climax as he had wished to see action. During formation-flying practice he became disillusioned with the official RAF guidelines, which decreed that pilots should fly line-astern and attack the enemy singly. He believed in attacking the enemy from all sides with as many aircraft as possible, but this tactic was not to be tested for some time.

At this time Bader crashed a Spitfire during take-off, committing the cardinal sin of forgetting to switch the propeller pitch to fine and hitting the ground at eighty miles per hour. Despite this elementary lapse he was promoted from Flying Officer to Flight Lieutenant and he joined 222 Squadron, also based at Duxford. A short time later the squadron moved to Kirton-in-Lindsay, but were still carrying out boring convoy patrols. However Bader was soon to get his first taste of combat as things were going badly for the BEF (British Expeditionary Force) and its allies in France, culminating in the evacuation of Dunkirk.

Squadrons were ordered to provide air cover for the retreating troops in their fleet of innumerable small ships and Bader recorded his first 'kill,' a Messerschmitt whose pilot's reactions were too slow. He was also credited with damaging a Heinkel and a Dornier, despite claiming five 'kills' in that particular conflict.

Following flying operations over Dunkirk, Douglas was posted once more, this time to Coltishall to command 242

Squadron as Squadron Leader. This squadron flew Hurricanes and was mainly made up of tough Canadians that had suffered high losses and whose morale was very low. They viewed their new commander with scepticism, particularly when they discovered he had tin legs! When Bader first encountered the pilots he received no respect from them and they virtually ignored him. Angered by this he stomped out of the dispersal hut and climbed into a Hurricane and performed non-stop aerobatics, like the early days at Hendon. He showed them that he was no passenger and the pilots were won over. It was then that Bader discovered they had been left to their own devices whilst fighting in France, separated from their ground staff and moved around from place to place. They were reduced to servicing their own aircraft with very few tools, scrounging food and even sleeping under the wing of their aircraft. Bader's reaction was to rejuvenate the pilots by providing badly needed uniforms, tools and spares. He also acquired two top-line Flight Commanders and turned the squadron into a first-class fighting unit.

It was learned that the German Luftwaffe were going all-out to achieve air superiority over Britain to allow the launch of 'Operation Sea Lion,' the invasion of Britain. Churchill's stirring speech spelt out the importance of maximum resistance:

The Battle of France is over. I expect that the Battle of Britain is about to begin. Upon that battle depends the survival of Christian civilisation. Let us therefore brace ourselves to our duty and so bear ourselves that if the British Commonwealth and Empire last for a thousand years men will say – this was their finest hour.

Bader and his squadron became part of the increased flying activity and he got the opportunity of much needed combat. In July Douglas recorded his first kill with his new squadron and further successes came in the days that followed. The Battle of Britain had begun and he was in his element, leading his rejuvenated pilots, who followed him without question and going 'hell for leather' at the enemy. His wife, Thelma, tried to curb his eagerness, pointing out that he was not immortal. 'Don't be damn silly darling,' was his reaction. 'I've got armour plate behind me, tin legs underneath and an engine in front. How are they going to get me?

His 'kill-count' rose dramatically during the hectic activity and at the height of the Battle of Britain, in mid-September, he was awarded the DSO (Distinguished Service Order) for his leadership in combat. During one mission Bader attacked a Heinkel, but found he had run out of ammunition. He was so incensed he even considered ramming the German aircraft, but satisfied himself by slicing off its rudder with his propeller.

During this period 11 Group, covering south-east England bore the brunt of the German attacks and 12 Group, which contained Bader's squadron, were sometimes held in readiness guarding the industrial heartland. At times 242 Squadron was called upon to assist 11 Group and they were shunted between Duxford and Coltishall.

At that time there was great excitement at an anti-aircraft battery unit close to Duxford that was instrumental in shooting down a German Dornier on the 23 August. The gun crew had started the day with another dawn 'stand-to' red alert, with little chance of action. As on many previous occasions the only likely excitement would be tracking yet another lost 'brylcream boy' (RAF pilot). The gun crew felt they were stranded and forgotten in the Cambridgeshire countryside as the war passed them by. Not since the outbreak of war, a full year earlier, had their guns been used in anger. Now, stuck on a road junction off the A 505, their role was to protect Duxford airfield.

There was one aspect of the engagement that was kept closely under wraps at the time. It was one of the first occasions that fledgling radar took part in targeting hostile aircraft for the guns. One such set of equipment was dumped on the battery and on this occasion it worked well as the radar team located the Dornier in the clouds and the bearing data was shouted to the gunners so that the guns were continuously pointing in the direction of the unseen target.

Unfortunately, radar for the guns was still in prototype form and could not detect the height or angle of the target, so they were aimed at a height of 20,000 feet, which was the cloud ceiling provided by the Met. Office. As soon as the Dornier reached a break in the clouds, shells were on the way in a split second before the aircraft could change course and there was the momentary flash of an explosion on its port engine. The aircraft climbed for a moment into the cloud cover, but reappeared falling steeply away on its port wing. The German pilot managed to regain control of the Dornier and it turned homewards with flames pouring from the port engine and damage to the tail unit. In a risky manoeuvre, the pilot put the plane into a steep dive and the fierce draught extinguished the flames. However, there was no relief for the stricken Dornier as it began to lose power in the starboard engine, which had probably been hit by shrapnel. The pilot ordered the jettisoning of its bombs over open farmland, before one of a stream of tracer shells fired from a Bofors site at Whittlesford hit the aircraft's fuselage. Machine gun fire inflicted further damage and the bomber made a forced belly-landing in a field.

The German crew escaped unscathed and tried to destroy the plane with detonators carried for such an emergency, but they failed to activate. The Germans were 'captured' by a part-time member of the West Suffolk Constabulary whose pitchfork and gun dog were not really required. Then a party of soldiers arrived and the handover of the prisoners was quite amicable. The Germans shared out chocolates and peppermints from their rations, whilst the British soldiers obtained tea and cigarettes for their prisoners. The German pilot peacefully shared a cigarette with a soldier and contemplated the absurdity of war!

A great supporter of his 12 Group commander, Air Vice Marshall Leigh-Mallory, Bader joined him as an advocate of the contentious 'Big Wing' premise, which caused a great deal of controversy within Fighter Command at that time. He advocated an aggressive form of tactics, which consisted of assembling large formations of defending fighters north of London ready to inflict maximum damage to the large German bomber formations as they approached via south-east England. Leigh-Mallory listened intently to Douglas' firmly-held views, but did not act on them immediately. He was opposed by others who were unconvinced of the effectiveness of such tactics, believing it would take too long to assemble so many aircraft and give much-needed support to the hard-pressed 11 Group.

Nevertheless, Bader's confidence was at full throttle and it impacted on the pilots of 242 Squadron, who held him in awe and admiration. He was the 'rock' that they clung to in those uncertain and frightening days, particularly the newcomers who were young and inexperienced. Statistics showed that the life expectancy of a fighter pilot was very short. His tactics that he had worked on with his pilots became gospel and Group even requested a report on how to break up an enemy formation. This extract from *Reach for the Sky* (Bader's life story by Paul Brickhill) explains:

They can be dispersed by shock tactics of the leading section fighters diving into their midst as close as possible . . . risk of collision is there, but the fact remains that the effect of a near collision makes German pilots take violent evasive action which, of course, immediately breaks up any tight formation. Apart from giving the fighters their chance, it also ruins the enemy's chance of accurate bombing.

This tactic worked so well that 242 Squadron were described by Leigh-Mallory as the 'disintegration squadron.'

Bader instilled into his pilots the three most important rules of the mantra regarding aerial combat. Gain height to attack your enemy from above. Get the sun behind you as this blinds the opponent and never fly straight and level for more than a few seconds.

About this time Douglas designed an emblem for the squadron, which depicted a caricature of Hitler being kicked in the rear by a flying boot labelled 242 and it was painted on the noses of all the Hurricanes. This helped the moral of the pilots whose lives were a terrifying contrast. Off duty in the evenings they could relax for a few hours with drinks, games and sing-songs in the pub, but come the morning the gut-wrenching ordeal of waiting at dispersal in readiness to fly into combat, possibly never to return, was played out. Bader never complained if a pilot let off steam vigorously, particularly at parties in the mess. One evening at such a boisterous event, Leigh-Mallory attended and entered the fray by performing a Highland Fling on a table!

Another form of light relief at that time was the awarding of nicknames to airfields by their occupants. They demonstrated the loathing of rain, mud and rural isolation suffered by RAF and American personnel. Duxford became known as 'The

Duckpond' and RAF Ludford Magna was referred to as 'Mudford Magna.' Pilots who were subjected to annoying features surrounding airfields, which made taking off and landing difficult, were also a target. A small wooded hill, perilously close to RAF Elgin earned the title 'Gremlin's Roost.'

At the end of August Bader was instructed by Leigh-Mallory to take 242 Squadron to Duxford and pick up two squadrons, 19 and 310, which he would lead, in addition to his own, as a trial of the 'Big Wing' theory. Pleased by Leigh-Mallory's support Douglas spent three days practicing formation-flying with his three squadrons, having 19 Squadron's Spitfires above and behind as they were faster than the Hurricanes.

The Luftwaffe was still ferociously attacking southern England and 11 Group were in the thick of the action. Douglas was itching for combat to try out his Wing but stuck to his task of training its thirty-six pilots. Leigh-Mallory himself visited Duxford to observe their practice and before leaving told Bader that the next time 11 Group called on their services he could take his whole team.

Next day the Luftwaffe turned on London and at last the Wing was scrambled and encountered around seventy Dorniers with Messerschmitt support flying about 5,000 feet above them. Anxious to gain height Douglas instructed his pilots to climb at full throttle. He did just that, but the squadrons were trailing behind him and they ended up as an untidy group of aircraft when it came to attacking the enemy. Even so during the combat 11 German aircraft were shot down, of which Bader got two, but was hit by cannon shell and managed to return to base.

Next morning the Wing was held in readiness as the German bombers hammered London and that afternoon Leigh-Mallory made an appearance. Douglas told him of their previous day's problems, that they were flying too low and the squadrons were kept on the ground too long. He also stressed that if they were alerted earlier they could be on top and ready for the attackers. Although radar could plot enemy aircraft assembling over France, 11 Group felt they should wait until the Germans approached, it was pointed out to him. 'However,' said Leigh-Mallory, 'Your Wing's score

Hurricanes based at RAF Duxford flying in formation

yesterday backs up the experiment, so carry on with it and we will endeavour to get you into the air faster.'

As Bader waited once again at Duxford with his three squadrons the following morning, word came from 'Ops.' of a build-up of German aircraft over the Pas de Calais. His chance came as the Wing was soon scrambled and this time made more of an impression in the ensuing aerial battle shooting down twenty of the enemy for the loss offour Hurricanes. However, Douglas remained unsatisfied and at the next opportunity of speaking to Leigh-Mallory he told him if they had deployed more fighters they would have had even greater success.

His words resulted in two further squadrons coming under Bader's command and shortly afterwards 302 and 611 flew into Duxford to be incorporated into what became known as '12 Group Wing.' Twice that day Douglas led a pack of sixty fighters on patrol above North London, but encountered no enemy aircraft.

At dawn on the morning of the 15th September, the five squadrons of the 12 Group Wing stood in readiness waiting for action on what would became known as 'Battle of Britain Day.'

*Pilots of 310 (Czechoslovak) Squadron at RAF Duxford
in 1940*

Enemy aircraft were reported to be approaching the channel and when the German bombers were over Kent, the shield of 11 Group squadrons was waiting for them and soon the fields were littered by the burning wrecks of German aircraft. Then there was relative silence with enemy bombers, some damaged, haring back over the Channel at top speed. However this was not the end of the battle as a further mass of bombers was discovered making for London.

A few minutes later the 12 Group Wing was scrambled and instructed to head south-east and patrol the Canterbury and Gravesend area. On arrival the three Hurricane squadrons climbed high above the clouds that blanketed much of the south-east with the Spitfires to the left and slightly above. Eventually, they caught sight of around forty Junkers and Dorniers below them. Initially, Bader thought they were unescorted, but soon caught sight of a band of Messerschmitts, into which he dived, guns blazing, through their front rank. All hell was let loose with aircraft darting in all directions and it was so hectic he saw a Spitfire and Dornier collide and fall to earth entangled. After several minutes of mayhem the sky miraculously cleared once more and the Wing headed for base.

A couple of hours later they were scrambled once more and told to patrol North Weald. Bader led his Wing through a gap in the clouds and found around forty bombers above them. Cursing his late arrival, Douglas cried, 'Break up!' and the sky was suddenly a mass of wheeling and jinking aircraft. Once again, after a short, hectic interval, the enemy disappeared and the Wing returned to base. This time there was no further scramble and night closed in.

Although the pilots thought nothing of it, the day was the greatest of the Battle of Britain. To them it was just another wearing day of tension and relief and the feeling that the Wing had earned its stripes by shooting down fifty-two enemy aircraft and eight probables. Leigh-Mallory was quick to congratulate Bader and his Wing and Douglas took the opportunity to suggest that if they had been scrambled earlier they could have wreaked even more damage on the enemy. He also added that he would like to shoot down a complete enemy raid, which amused Leigh-Mallory.

Bader nearly got his chance to do so some time later when the Wing was scrambled to confront forty plus bombers over the Thames near Gravesend and he found there were more RAF aircraft than those of the enemy. Not only that, but there were no German fighters. Douglas and his pilots had a field day and the scattered bombers turned tail for France. This time the enemy was unlucky and the sky was soon filled with parachutes and burning bombers. None of the Wing's pilots had ever seen so many parachutes and their achievements were reached without a single casualty.

Desperation was apparent in the enemy's next moves. Tactics were disjointed with fighters sent in advance of bombers to draw RAF fighters up and exhaust their fuel supply. Daylight bombing had shrunk to virtually nothing, but occasionally German aircraft fought their way through to London, but without much success. Attacks on the south-east continued, well away from 12 Group and Bader became frustrated once more with the absence of opponents. The Wing was scrambled a couple of times most days, but did not encounter any opposition. Despite the lack of action Bader had become famous. Too wrapped up in running the Wing to notice, he was happy in the knowledge that his pilots' morale was very high, although that was due to the man himself. He exuded a cheerful confidence, which impacted on them, particularly his carefree repartee, during sorties, with the Ops. Controller, Wing Commander 'Woodie' Woodhall. An example went something like this:

'Hey, Woodie, I've got an appointment in an hour for a game of squash, ring Squadron Leader Price and tell him I'll be late.' Woodhall, 'Sorry, I'm busy. There is a war on you know.' Bader, 'Just pick up one of your phones, it won't take a minute.' Woodhall, 'Okay. Okay, I will, just this once.' Bader, 'Good Man.' Woodhall, 'Would you mind finding the enemy now?'

Who was to say that some of this banter was not designed to relieve the tension of the pilots listening on the R/T. It helped to build up the confidence of new pilots thrown into this maelstrom of warfare.

The mainly futile patrols continued until 27th September when an untidy formation of around thirty Messerschmitts was encountered wheeling around Dover. The 12 Group Wing tore into them and downed twelve, whilst Bader's windscreen was covered in oil streaming from a damaged Messerschmitt that he was chasing. The enemy escaped retribution when Douglas had the aircraft in his sights, despite the oil deposit, and found that his guns were out of ammunition.

After that the bombers appeared even less frequently and the fighters took to darting over London and other areas with small bombs attached to their undersides, but their effect was minimal. For the next fortnight the Wing assembled at Duxford each day and patrolled over London, but the skies remained clear. The Germans had run out of time and on the 12th October, Operation Sea Lion was postponed. It was once again Winston Churchill who spread the significance of this triumph in his immortal words:

Never in the field of human conflict has so much been owed by so many to so few.

In December 1940 Douglas was awarded the DFC (Distinguished Flying Cross) to add to his DSO. It was given for his services during the Battle of Britain, during which 242 Squadron had claimed 62 victories and the 12 Group Wing 152.

After a period of calm the peace was shattered by German bombers going full pelt at London and other major cities during the night. It was the beginning of the Blitz, when the will and resistance of the British people, particularly Londoners, was under threat. During this time Leigh-Mallory was moved to 11 Group and swiftly arranged for 242 Squadron to join him.

Then began the process of turning defence into attack by sending squadrons over France, initially, bombers escorted by a pack of fighters. Not a lot came of this, but Bader was kept busy with a routine of convoy patrols, formation-flying and searching for enemy aircraft.

In March 1941 Leigh-Mallory sent for Douglas to inform him that ideas were being worked on for carrying the attack to France with more ambitious sweeps than the previous ones. In order to do this it was planned to appoint Wing Commanders on certain stations to organize and lead Wings there. Bader was told that he was to be one of those Wing Commanders and that he was going to Tangmere once more. This news delighted him, but the only fly in the ointment was that 242 Squadron would have to be left behind. He was placated somewhat by the news that he would be leading three Spitfire squadrons, one of which had been in 12 Group Wing. Woodhall, newly promoted to Group Captain, was also transferred to Tangmere to take over the station and also act as Controller. Leigh-Mallory wanted his established team together. Bader had his initials 'DB' painted on the side of his aircraft for ease of identification and Woodhall jokingly christened him 'Dogsbody.' The name stuck and even became his call-sign.

Between March and August 1941 Bader took part in sixty-two fighter sweeps over France and seemed untouchable to all around him. He was much luckier than many pilots who lost their lives or were badly wounded in combat. Flying Officer Jimmie Coward, flying from Fowlmere, Duxford's satellite airfield in Cambridgeshire, was piloting one of the few cannon-equipped Spitfires in the RAF when disaster struck. As he led his section into battle against a pack of Dorniers, his cannons jammed and, simultaneously, his aircraft shuddered violently.

Coward suddenly felt a dull pain, like a kick on the shin in a rugby scrum, then saw to his terror that his bare left foot was lying on the cockpit floor, severed from his leg by all but a few ligaments. He managed to nurse the stricken Spitfire to within sight of Duxford until it dived out of control. Coward bailed out with ease, but the agony of his foot spinning crazily by its ligaments drove him to desperate action. Pulling the ripcord, he began to float earthwards from 20,000 feet, but blood was spurting from a severed artery and vanishing in thin swirls far below him. The slipstream had sucked away his gloves, and his hands, blue with cold, could not release the clamp of his parachute harness in order for him to reach the first-aid kit in his breast pocket. He realised that if he was to survive, he had to improvise a tourniquet quickly. Frantically, fumbling with numbed fingers, he managed to open the strap and buckle of his flying helmet, to which his radio telephone lead was still attached. Then, raising his damaged leg almost to his chin, he bound the lead tightly round his thigh, choking the flow of blood. The immediate danger stifled, he drifted slowly across Duxford airfield, landing on the grass. Within the hour, Coward was in a Cambridge hospital where his damaged leg was amputated below the knee, a similar fate to that which Bader had suffered, though not so dire.

Such a disaster was far from Douglas's mind at that time. Returning over the Channel one day, 'Cocky' Dundas, one of Douglas's pilots, was shaken by the sight of Bader, flying alongside, push back his cockpit hood, unclip his oxygen mask and stick his pipe in his mouth. Unbelievably, holding the joystick between his knees, he proceeded to light his pipe and sit there sending puffs of smoke into the air. Dundas liked a cigarette himself, but he reckoned no normal pilot lit a match or cigarette lighter in the cockpit. Bader looked across at him, grinned and made a rude gesture. From then on Bader regularly enjoyed a smoke on returning to base and his pilots flying alongside would pull away from him, half jokingly and half serious, in case Douglas's Spitfire exploded!

On one occasion Bader fired at three Messerschmitts, but they sheared off and left him. Two more pounced on him and he shot down one of them. When he returned to base he claimed one aircraft destroyed and three frightened. A message arrived from Group Headquarters demanding to know what he meant and they were not amused by his answer. Another message, this time from Leigh-Mallory, arrived informing Douglas of the award of a Bar to his DSO.

Douglas carried on with his pot-shots at authority and even occasionally indulged in forbidden aerobatics over Tangmere airfield, warning his pilots against doing the same. He told offenders not to do it, as he had lost his legs doing it and more experienced pilots than them had died doing it. 'When you are Wing Commanders you can do it,' he told them, 'but until then, obey the rules!'

By this time Bader had done more sweeps than any other pilot and still insisted on leading the Wing on every raid. In a way he overdid the personal leadership, thus there was no one trained to follow him. This became only too true when in August of that year his long run of luck ran out. Just after crossing the French coast during a search for German fighters they encountered a group of Messerschmitts dead ahead and about 2,000 feet below; sitting targets. Homing in on one of them he suddenly realised that in his eagerness he was about to collide with it and pulled away quickly. Cursing his stupidity, he found himself separated from his Wing and was astounded by the sight of six Messerschmitts ahead unaware of his presence. He should have resisted the urge to fire at the sitting ducks, but, in contrast to what he drilled into his pilots, he did not. Remarkably, he shot down two of them before being menaced by a further two. He paid for his recklessness by pulling away sharply and colliding with another aircraft. The whole of his Spitfire behind the cockpit was sheared off and the nose section plunged earthwards. In a panic Douglas tore his helmet and mask off and jettisoned the cockpit hood, but rather than pulling himself clear of the remnant of his aircraft he found one of his legs jammed and he could not release it. Down he went with the broken Spitfire dragging him by the leg until suddenly something snapped and he was plucked from the plane. He pulled on his ripcord and mercifully, his parachute opened and he floated peacefully towards the ground. Something flapped in his face, it was his trouser leg. He had lost his right leg! A silly thought crossed his mind. How lucky he was to have lost the trapped artificial leg. He would not have survived otherwise. The ground was fast approaching and he landed heavily in a field, feeling some of his ribs buckle before passing out.

When he came round three German soldiers were bending over him. They picked him up and carried him to a car. He was ferried to a hospital in a semi-conscious state, to be examined by a doctor, who was amazed when he removed Bader's trousers. 'We have heard about you,' he exclaimed. At Bader's request to know where he was the doctor replied, 'A hospital in St.Omer.'

Later, as he lay in bed, his whole body ached and every time he moved it felt like a knife being stuck below his heart, but his befogged mind was not capable of grasping its significance. When his mind finally began to clear he thought of Thelma and the pilots of the Wing, hoping that one of them had seen him bale out. Unfortunately, no one had and there was stunned disbelief back at Tangmere when he did not return.

Next morning Douglas was feeling stronger and his first thought was to get word to Thelma and acquire legs. He was visited by German pilots from nearby St. Omer airfield and eventually a Luftwaffe officer informed him that his leg had been found. At his call a jackbooted soldier stomped to Bader's bedside holding his missing right leg, covered in mud. Douglas was delighted, but then noticed that it was badly damaged. He turned on the charm. 'Could you possibly get your men at the airfield to repair it for me?' It worked, for it was not long before the officer and the jack-booted soldier returned with his beautifully restored leg. It was a magnificent feat of engineering and Douglas thanked the officer profusely.

It was not long before Bader was itching to escape and get back to England. A chance arose when he was invited to visit Adolf Galland, a German fighter ace, at Wissant. During the visit he was allowed to sit in the cockpit of a Messerschmitt whilst Galland pointed out its salient features. Douglas had the irrational thought of starting the engine and taking off, but resisted it.

Anxious to see the lie of the land Bader looked over the

Squadron Leader (later Group Captain) Douglas Bader with Alexander 'Sasha' Hess Commanding Officer of 310 (Czechoslovak) Squadron at RAF Duxford in 1940

countryside and saw that he was close to the sea. He even imagined he could see the white cliffs of Dover and longed for them to leave him alone for long enough to climb into the Messerschmitt again and return to Tangmere. After the war Galland sent a photograph to Bader, of him sitting in the cockpit of the aircraft, on which he noticed a German officer standing beside the plane holding a pistol!

On his return to hospital he was instructed to be ready the following morning to be taken to Germany. It came as a bolt from the blue and Douglas decided that he must escape that very night. With the aid of knotted bed sheets he lowered himself to the ground under cover of darkness and got through the gates without discovery. A French agent was waiting across the road to accompany him through the town, a journey which seemed interminable and his stumps became so horribly chafed he had to be virtually carried for the last section. He was taken to a safe house where he was given a bed for the night.

Next day at noon Bader heard the familiar drone of aircraft

RAF Duxford, 2 'riggers' examine damage to an aircraft

and what he did not see was the long box fall by parachute as flak burst around it. Unbeknown to Bader it was a spare leg sent by the RAF and sanctioned by Goering himself.

At half-past five that day the house was searched by German troops and Bader hid in a shed in the back garden. Unfortunately, he was discovered lying under straw and baskets. In fact he was lucky to survive for the soldier who found him had kicked aside the baskets and was bayoneting the straw. He swore that the occupants of the house knew nothing of his presence and that he had crept into the shed during the night.

Bader was taken to Headquarters where he was questioned, but he gave no answers. He was then taken to another room where he was delighted to find the box containing his spare leg. Then they made him unstrap his legs and took them away until the following morning when he was carried from the building to a waiting ambulance. He was taken to Brussels where he was carried once more onto a train bound for Germany and put into a compartment with his legs stored in a rack above him.

He reached Frankfurt at midnight and was driven by car

to Dulag Luft, the reception and interrogation centre for RAF prisoners. The following morning he was questioned and given a false form with a red cross at its head that the Germans always used. Bader entered his name rank and number on it and handed it back, refusing anything further. He was placed in a compound with other prisoners and given his legs back. It was not long before Douglas became involved in an escape plan, but before he could take part in the actual event he was moved to Brussels to appear before a court-martial. It turned out to be for the doctor and some of the staff from the hospital at St. Omer that Bader refused to incriminate.

Bader was returned to Dulag Luft, but only remained there for a short time before he was transferred for insubordination. This time it was to Lubeck and the wire compound of Oflag VIB where he joined 400 emaciated British officers. Food was terrible and scarce and the Commandant had no time for the Geneva Convention.

Sometime later all the prisoners were taken to another camp at Warburg where the Germans were concentrating all British officers. During the journey several officers managed to cut a hole in the floor of a truck at night and escape into the darkness. Bader was very envious until he learned that one escapee was killed by the train.

3,000 prisoners were held in squalor in the cage at Warburg, although they were allowed food parcels which gave them a decent meal every day. The compound had an open area where prisoners played 'rugger' (rugby) and Douglas found it was no longer excruciating to watch and not be able to take part. He was a most vociferous onlooker. One bright spot during the boring and frustrating days of confinement was the receipt of a letter from Thelma, which said he was sadly missed by the Wing, according to Woodhall. It also contained the splendid news that he had been awarded a Bar to his DFC.

The escape committee was active at Warburg. Several tunnels were dug by eager participants, but the Germans always found and wrecked them. Bader's only outlet was 'goon-baiting,' (taunting his captors) and even goading them into drawing their pistols in fury. After two abortive attempts to escape, one through a tunnel and the other from a clothing hut just outside the barbed-wire gate, from which he managed to get outside the camp before being recaptured. Douglas took part in hatching a plan to escape from the cell block, but the plotters decided to wait until winter was over. Unfortunately, before the attempt could be made, Bader was amongst a party of Air Force officers that were moved to another camp, between Berlin and Breslau, Stalag Luft III. Here he met Harry Day and Bob Tuck, two of his old chums. Bader was still burning to escape and, despite several other tunnels already in the process of being dug, he went before the escape committee with a scheme for digging a short tunnel, begun near the warning wire, in a single night. To his annoyance, Douglas's idea was turned down.

The baiting campaign worsened and Bader, by his belligerence and the others' goading of the Germans, resulted in the loss of certain privileges. Things came to a head when Douglas was told he would be leaving the camp the following day. He was incensed by this and refused to go, which nearly ended with him being shot, but he stuck to his guns and stayed in his hut the next day. As evening drew near a group of over fifty guards, in battle-order and with fixed bayonets, marched from the administrative compound towards the barbed wire, followed by the Commandant accompanied by many of his officers. The prisoners massed behind the wire and the air was electric. Group Captain Massey, the senior officer, talked to the Commandant by the gate before going into Bader's hut.

A few minutes later Bader appeared and stomped to the gate, which was opened to allow him through. His change of heart had been due to Group Captain Massey's warning that he could spark an incident in which there could be casualties. Goading to the last, Douglas passed along the line of troops outside the gate looking intently at their appearance, as if inspecting them! Suddenly, the tension was deflated and the sight of a lone and legless officer being accompanied from the camp by nearly sixty armed soldiers became laughable.

Bader's new 'abode' was Stalag VIIIB, Lamsdorf, where over 20,000 soldiers were being held. Here he was assigned to sick quarters, a hut in a separate cage near the main gate, with another prisoner, a Flight Lieutenant who required special treatment for a damaged foot. A few days later they watched through a window as a group of prisoners marched out of the main gate. Bader asked an RAMC doctor where they were heading. He was told it was just a working party off to a nearby town. It might be easy to escape from such a party Bader thought and put the suggestion to the doctor. 'It's dead easy,' was his reply. 'We could get you two on one if you are really interested.' This was good news and Douglas put the suggestion to the escape committee. Although it was deemed difficult with his artificial legs, they said they would try and think of something.

Bader and the Flight Lieutenant heard nothing for three boring weeks before they got word that there would be an attempt to smuggle the two of them out in the midst of a light working party bound for an aerodrome at Gleiwitz on the German-Polish border, the following morning. They were provided with brooms and army battledress to help them get off camp and next morning a plan was put into action. All the prisoners in the working parties were stripped and searched in a hut next to the sick quarters before being allowed through the main gate. This was avoided by a clever deception. Bader and his friend lounged on the front step of the sick bay the next morning and when the working party passed them all its members were taken into the adjacent hut to be searched. Bader and his companion picked up their brooms sauntered into the road and started sweeping. As the working party and their escort emerged from the hut, the last man out dropped his kit and started swearing loudly. The guards looked on and laughed at the fellow's so-called misfortune. Whilst the guards were distracted, Bader and his companion swept their way into the middle of the working party and handed their brooms to two of the men, who swept languidly through the group and back towards the compound. The man who had dropped his kit picked it up and the party marched up to the main gate. Their heads were counted before allowing them through it and as they marched away some of the men clustered round the two escapees. Someone took Bader's kitbag and they marched to a waiting train that took them to Gleiwitz. It was a two-mile walk from the station to what looked like a military camp. By this time Douglas was nearly all in and just managed to ask one of the prisoners that came to greet them, 'Where's the Aerodrome?' He was told it was a mile away and that they were never allowed there. What a tragedy! Bader, although in great pain and exhausted was forced to hobble to his new quarters, a room that he shared with two companions. He lay on his bunk and contemplated his next move, but the options seemed extremely limited.

Another problem awaited him the following morning as he learned that the prisoners had to do hard manual labour at this camp, which was beyond his capability. However, he was told he could be latrine man and clean out the toilets, which he accepted and found, ridiculously, that he quite enjoyed. Restless as ever, Bader began hatching another escape plan with three comrades, but before it could be put into practice, a bombshell occurred. All the prisoners were ordered to form up in the compound and, having done so, were given the absurd order to take their trousers down. The men who did not know Bader, began laughing and cheering, but he realised what was coming. With no chance of escape he limped to the German officer who had given the order and said, 'I am the man you are looking for.'

He was taken back to Lamsdorf where the Kommandant gave him a furious tongue-lashing, but as he did so Bader began to giggle. This made the Kommandant apoplectic and Douglas was sent to the cells and given ten days solitary confinement. On the ninth day the Kommandant entered his cell and informed him that he was to be transferred to the officer prison at Colditz Castle. They both knew that Colditz was the last stop for troublemakers and was escape-proof, which was no laughing matter.

When Bader arrived at the castle and heard the massive doors close behind him a sense of doom overcame him and when he was shown a small, stone cell he was horrified. However, before he could enter, a familiar voice assailed him. It was none other than his friend from the Hendon days, Geoffrey Stephenson. After warm greetings Douglas inquired if the prisoners lived in cells like the one he was about to enter. Thankfully, his friend said it would be just for that night and he would be able to join the others the following day. Feeling much improved, Bader entered the cell without opposition.

The following day he was let out, photographed and fingerprinted before being allowed to join Stephenson who led him to a large upstairs room with a window overlooking the inner courtyard. The place seemed quite acceptable, in fact it was the best quarters he had been given since his capture. He shared it with three army officers, one of whom he already knew. Conditions were decent, including a good supply of Red Cross food parcels and the use of a bath. What a luxury after having been denied one for more than a year. After a tour of the prisoners' section of the castle he was not so thrilled, noting the grimness of the surroundings and the only shared recreation area was the small inner courtyard, around which soared walls seventy feet high. As for the exterior, the castle seemed escape-proof. Its walls were ninety feet high and seven feet thick and they perched on a one hundred feet high cliff. The only way out was a road from the castle and to get to it the prisoners had to pass through the other part of the castle where the Germans were quartered.

After a talk with two members of the escape committee, his worst fears were realised. Every prisoner was an avid escaper, but only a handful had ever been successful at Colditz. Many ideas and ingenious schemes were constantly being envisaged, but none ever came to anything. Disheartened, Bader settled into the routine of Colditz, long days when you could do little but sit around, gaze out of the window, wander around the courtyard, or read. The monotony gnawed at Douglas who returned to his hobby of 'goon-baiting' and was joined vociferously by the other prisoners. His insubordination knew no bounds and his main targets were the security officer, and the Deputy Kommandant who wore a conspicuous cloak that made him a figure of fun. Bader's favourite trick was to pass him and blow smoke past the officer's cheek, until the German confronted him with the news that life would be easier if he set a better example to his fellow prisoners, which, of course, Bader ignored.

Things came to a head when he and a fellow prisoner tried to smuggle out a message written inside a photograph slit in two and re-sealed. It contained a little information regarding all they knew about the situation in Germany, such as the effects of the bombing by the Allies and the movement of German troops. Unfortunately, it was discovered by the Germans and Douglas was taken for interrogation to Leipzig where he was accused of inciting mutiny and even of espionage. In possession of the information contained in the split photograph, the interrogator informed him that it constituted espionage and he could be shot. He was warned that he would have to attend a war court in Berlin.

This warning prompted Bader to resume his attempt to escape and thereby miss his appointment in Berlin. Two further plans were concocted, the first being an outlandish one of crawling onto the roof and edging around it until they could drop into the German part of the castle. By climbing over more roofs and sliding down one of the cables securing a lightning conductor they could reach the top of the cliff. From there, with the use of a rope, they would lower themselves forty feet into the bed of the moat, which, fortunately, was dry. All that remained from that point was to climb over barbed wire fences and terraces planted with mines before fleeing from the castle. Thankfully, the madcap scheme was aborted by the escape committee, who explained it would be a severe test for a fit and athletic man, and on no account should Bader attempt it.

Still determined to escape Bader joined some Polish prisoners who were trying to find an escape route through the sewer pipes. One of the Poles gained access to several, but found that most were tapered until they were so small in diameter a person would get stuck in them. The remainder came to a dead end.

Defeated at last Bader realised further attempts at escape were futile and resigned himself to spending the rest of the war in the castle. His disappointment and frustration were alleviated to some extent by letters and books sent by Thelma. He even became a great fan of the poet Swinburne.

As Douglas feared, he remained at Colditz until it was relieved by the Allies near the end of the war. After his return to England he was given the honour of leading a victory fly-past of 300 aircraft over London in 1945. He was officially credited with twenty-two and a half kills, but he always

RAF Duxford sector 'G' Operations (Op's) Room during World War Two

reckoned the figure was actually thirty.

Years later, whilst I was walking through north-west Scotland I was reminded of Bader by two incidents on my journey. The area in question, Wester Ross and Sutherland, is among the loneliest and most inhospitable in Britain. It is nearly denuded of people, thanks to the Highland Clearances of the early eighteen-hundreds when the lairds evicted the crofters from their lands to make way for sheep, which were more profitable.

My tale begins on leaving the village of Ullapool and heading north for Durness, near Cape Wrath. I described it in one of my books concerning long-distance walking and it runs thus:

The day began poorly and went downhill. I left Ullapool beneath heavy skies and spitting rain, cursing the weather. As I followed the road out of the village I was seeking a path that would lead me into the hills overlooking Strath Kinnaird. This particular thoroughfare looked promising on the map, for it cuts out a broad loop in the only road heading north from Ullapool, the A835.

I found the path about a mile from the village, which was a

RAF Duxford Station Commander A.B. (Woody) Woodhall

signal for the rain to switch to overdrive and a thick 'pea-souper' to obliterate any landmarks. In a few minutes I was wet through and with visibility down to a few yards I struggled to keep sight of the inconspicuous path, frequently resorting to my compass in order to stay on its line. I suffered some anxious moments until I met the track for which I was aiming. Relief flooded through me, for I now had a lifeline and would soon be in Strath Kannaird, or so I thought. My pace quickened as I ventured through a silent, ethereal world but, imagine my shock when the track abruptly disappeared into an expanse of water that lay across my path. I scanned the map, anxiously trying to pinpoint my position, only to find that I had walked off one map and nearly onto the next one, which unfortunately did not exactly correspond. Two miles of my route were missing and I had no idea what lay directly ahead. How far the water extended was impossible to assess, due to the murk and it seemed risky to try and walk round the obstruction, for I might lose my bearings in the fog. The only sensible solution was to backtrack several miles to the A835 road and take the longer route to Strath Kannaird. Angrily, I turned on my heel and did *just that, seething with frustration.*

I rejoined the road a mere mile farther on than where I had left it over two hours previously. During its passage the A835 road weaves through Strath Kannaird and onwards to Drumrunie and Elphin. As I trudged along it I became acquainted with the strategic tourist corridor that extends for over sixty miles to Durness on the north coast. It searches out gaps in the hills and glides over a rocky bed through the arid desert that is Sutherland. Eight miles of tarmac-crunching brought me to Drumrunie and almost to the border of Britain's farthest-flung county that boasts over three hundred lochs.

Not in the best of moods and thoroughly drenched I tramped through the tiny settlement of Drumrunie in an incessant downpour. As I squelched from the hamlet through a gap in the hills I relieved the drudgery of rain-soaked miles by giving free rein to my imagination. I became immersed in the exciting world depicted in Reach for the Sky, its well-thumbed pages being one of my favourite reads. It is the life story of Sir Douglas Bader who demonstrated such bravery and sheer guts to overcome his handicap.

I was mentally flailing around the skies, shooting down enemy aircraft with reckless courage, as Bader had done, when I was jerked from my daydream by a screech of brakes. A Landrover lurched to a stop beside me and a cheery young farmer shouted through the open window to inquire if I wanted a lift. What a temptation! Here was a golden opportunity to speed through the murk and gobble up the remaining miles to my night's destination. Then I thought of Bader. He would not have taken the soft option. Stoically, I declined the man's invitation, which prompted a retort that I must be mad; a logical conclusion when your kindness is rebuffed by a bedraggled walker dripping water from every pore. He roared away in a cloud of spray leaving me to savour a solitary crumb of comfort; Bader would have been proud of me!

The following day's walk took me from Elphin to Kylesku with the mist refusing to retreat and the weather remained stubbornly foul on the final stretch to Durness. Consequently, I stuck to the road for the whole three days. On the third day I passed through Laxford Bridge and headed for Rhiconich the next pocket of habitation, five miles to the north. The feeling of isolation returned as I followed a differently numbered, but equally contorted road. No walkers had been encountered and none were expected in the wild conditions that only an idiot would tolerate.

The only visible relief from the monotony was the occasional cluster of roadside flowers. Splashes of flag irises and bog myrtle were nectar to a man figuratively dying of thirst. Suddenly the silence was broken by the sound of an approaching vehicle and a car pulled up beside me. Its occupants were Japanese and the driver, who spoke perfect English, inquired politely if I would like a lift. Wouldn't I just! Then Bader took control once more and I heard myself refusing his generous offer. This caused a stir amongst the car's passengers, who gabbled animatedly in Japanese, throwing disbelieving glances in my direction. They obviously could not comprehend this crazy Englishman who chose to walk through the middle of nowhere in such weather. With a shrug of his shoulders the driver pulled away, bent on discovering more of Scotland in impenetrable mist. As the sound of the engine drifted away the door of my murky prison slammed shut once more and I began to doubt my purism.'

To continue the history of RAF Duxford, in October 1942 the first Americans arrived as Fighter Group 350 with Bell P-39 Airacobras and Spitfires, prior to heading out to join the 12th Air Force in North Africa. RAF Duxford was fully handed over to the United States 8th Air Force in April 1943 and became their Base 357. It consisted of three squadrons - 82,83 and 84, and the headquarters of the 78th Fighter Group who were officially welcomed by King George VI and Queen Elizabeth when they visited the airfield on 26 May 1943.

The 78th Fighter Group flew Mustangs and Thunderbolts during 1944 and acted as fighter escort on large daylight bomber raids in occupied Europe and Germany itself. They also undertook sweeps over hostile territory and became skilled at strafing; flying into targets at very low level to destroy ground installations. On D-Day, the 6th June 1944 during the beginning of the Allied invasion of occupied Europe, every available Thunderbolt was providing cover to the Allied invasion fleet as it crossed the Channel. Later the Group took part in raids on railway targets ahead of the ground forces.

The 78th served with distinction during the latter phase of World War Two and was credited with the destruction of 697 German aircraft before hostilities ended. Also during the Group's tenure at Duxford the airfield was visited by several famous film stars, including Bob Hope, Francis Langford and James Cagney. The Fighter Group formed a bond during their tenure with the local population, performing several good deeds for their benefit. One of these was the holding of Christmas parties for local children and the Americans' kindness was also extended to improving the lives of seven of their number who had lost one or both parents during hostilities. These local children were 'adopted' by American units, which consisted of 400 dollars gifted to each child to pay for their schooling and two meals a day for four years.

On Christmas Eve 1943 a party was arranged by the Fighter Group to be held at the Guildhall in Cambridge. The 78th's own 'Thunderbolt' dance band provided the music and the celebration was broadcast on the radio in the USA.

The most terrible accident of Duxford's history occurred in July 1944 when the American pilot of a B17 aircraft was persuaded to give rides and during strictly illegal low-level passes across the airfield, the aircraft struck one of the hangars, smashed into the 83 Squadron barracks and exploded. All its occupants were killed and the resulting fire lasted for three hours before it was extinguished. Fortunately, the barracks were almost empty at the time and only one man on the ground perished. Despite this tragedy the American Fighter Group's time at Duxford was an enjoyable one, referring to their period of occupation as 'taking over one of the finest and most comfortable bases of any station overseas.'

After the Second World War, in December 1945, the airfield was transferred back to the RAF and the following January 165 Squadron, equipped with Spitfires, returned to the station.

By 1947 the Spitfires were gone and were superseded by Gloster Meteor jet aircraft. However, the runway was still a grass one, overlaid by a perforated metal mesh laid by the Americans for use by their Thunderbolt aircraft. This had required constant attention and it was decided to build a completely new longer runway and taxiways. On completion of these facilities in 1951 the airfield became fully equipped with a new 6,000 feet runway and servicing platforms that allowed it to operate as a base for modern aircraft. Consequently, the Meteors of 64 and 65 Squadrons returned after the runway's construction and another hangar was erected alongside the four First World War hangars.

By 1954 Hawker Hunters had entered service as day fighters. 65 Squadron was equipped with them and the Hunter's versatility and excellent handling made it one of the outstanding British post-war fighters.

In 1956 the Gloster Javelin became the last of this type of fighter to enter service with the RAF and it lasted until 1968 with the disbandment of 60 Squadron at RAF Tengah. The closest the aircraft came to combat was during the Malaysian confrontation with Indonesia in the mid-nineteen-sixties. 64 Squadron operated these night fighters when Duxford was entering its final operational phase, for the defensive requirements that had initiated the fighter station coming into being no longer applied. The airfield was too far south and too far inland and the expensive improvements required for supersonic fighters could not be justified.

Duxford was closed as an RAF station in 1961 following the last operational RAF flight in July of that year. Decay began to overtake the site, with grass and weeds relentlessly encroaching on the airfield. The hangars and other buildings stood empty, but the married quarters and officers' quarters across the road from the airfield itself remained in use. Security was minimal and the airfield site was open to anyone wishing to use it for activities such as car and motor-cycle racing on its runway and perimeter track.

However, the station had a temporary reprieve in 1968 when it came into use for filming *The Battle of Britain*, as mentioned previously, when the airfield was leased to Spitfire Productions. The idea for a film about the Battle of Britain was the brainchild of film producer Benjamin Fisz, an ex-Polish Air Force Spitfire pilot. He was joined by Harry Saltzman and they set up Spitfire Productions Ltd.

King George VI and Queen Elizabeth visiting USAAF Duxford in 1943

and engaged United Artists to shoot the film. Harry Saltzman knew of Duxford and it was found to be a good location due to it retaining much of its wartime constitution, which included generous hangars, ample living accommodation and engineering workshops just across the road from the airfield.

In the spring of 1968 United Artists moved in and began restoration of the airfield which cost £38,000, including a tidy up and the application of camouflage on the hangars and other buildings.

As the script began to take shape it was realised that a large number of aircraft would be needed and the task of unearthing them fell to Group Captain Hamish Mahaddie, a much-decorated World War Two bomber pilot, who specialised in buying aircraft for film work. He began to comb the world for suitable Spitfires that were capable of looking like operational aircraft and he managed to procure twenty-seven that could be used for active filming and several more that could be used for static shots and spares. Hurricanes, real and replica, were placed around a section of the airfield arranged to resemble a BEF (British

Air Day at IWM Duxford in 1975

Expeditionary Force) airfield during withdrawal from France in 1940. For Luftwaffe aircraft, Mahaddie contacted the Spanish Air Force that was still using Messerschmitts and Heinkels. Around fifty Heinkels were loaned to United Artists by the Spanish Air Force and twenty-eight Messerschmitts were purchased that were being decommissioned.

During filming, Duxford required a large contingent of police to control the hoards of sightseers that trampled surrounding cornfields in order to watch proceedings and the planes in action. The south-west end of Duxford airfield doubled for France with a mock-up of a French chateau, the structure having front and sides only and the area also housed tents and other equipment.

By strategic placement of cameras Duxford portrayed two airfields and the bombing raid by the Germans formed one of the most exciting scenes of the film. Unfortunately, the film company had not been granted definite permission to destroy a hangar depicted in it, but by good or bad fortune, whichever you wish to look at it, the hangar disappeared in a fireball and massive plumes of smoke during filming!

In 1968 the Ministry of Defence put the airfield up for tender and various plans were submitted, including those of a sports and leisure complex and two prisons. A further suggestion was returning the land to farming, or creating a country park. All these proposals were discarded, thankfully. By 1971 a public enquiry into the proposed use of the site was carried out and at that time the Imperial War Museum was searching for a suitable site for the storage, restoration and display of aircraft that were too large for its headquarters in London. Consequently, the Museum sought to use Duxford airfield for this purpose and by autumn of that year permission was granted for the Museum and the East Anglian Aviation Society to use part of the airfield and to house historic aircraft. The first plane was acquired in 1972, a Royal Navy Sea Vixen and later other aircraft and historic exhibits arrived, enough to allow the opening of the site in October 1973 for a special Air Day. This was a very successful event, which probably led to the Ministry of Defence, at the conclusion of the public enquiry in 1975, granting the Imperial War Museum full use of Duxford airfield as a branch of its operations.

The Department of the Environment was given the assignment of restoring buildings and the hangars. Due to a disagreement the East Anglian Aviation Society moved its collection to Bassingbourn, but some of its members remained and formed the Duxford Aviation Society that forged a strong link with the Museum. Its members gave invaluable assistance with the restoration of aircraft and vehicles.

In 1975 a two-day display was organised by the two bodies, which was very well attended and included air displays by several aircraft. In June 1976 the Imperial War Museum Duxford collection had grown to such a size that it was decided to open the airfield on a daily basis and public support was greater than anticipated. However, there was one 'fly in the ointment,' in the shape of the M11 motorway that required 150 acres of the airfield's land and reduced the length of the usable runway by 1500 feet.

An event in August 1977 caused a great deal of excitement and publicity; the arrival of Concorde - the innovative aircraft of its day. This helped to increase visitor numbers and by 1980 more than a million had attended. In addition more aircraft had arrived, resulting in the provision of a new hangar.

I was amongst the million or so visitors as I paid a nostalgic visit, my first since leaving the RAF, in 1980 to view the assortment of aircraft that was being gathered from around the world for restoration and to see the aircraft on display. It was quite an eye-opener to find the variety of planes on view, many requiring considerable refurbishment, involving substantial cost. Also, it was good to see my old station take on a new lease of life and aircraft return, albeit not on active service. Apparently, Duxford is now the best preserved World War Two airfield in Europe.

The highlight of my tour of the airfield was to climb aboard the magnificent pre-production Concorde, one of the most recognisable passenger aeroplanes ever built. Unfortunately, it remained merely on view on the ground. What a great pity, for I would have loved a trip in that sleek and inspirational aircraft, built with the combined skills of the British and the French.

I took the opportunity to visit the station buildings across the road from the airfield, which awakened other memories of my time at Duxford. As I passed through the main gate my mind flashed back to the first time I had entered the aerodrome that February evening in 1958 with everything under the cover of darkness, unfamiliar and a little daunting. In 1980 the living quarters looked just the same, austere regulation buildings that characterised all RAF stations. The largest of the other buildings that had comprised the NAAFI and the dining hall overlooked the main parade ground. In one of the photographic displays at the airfield I had seen that parade square occupied by all the personnel at RAF Duxford during the final inspection parade marking the closure of the station in October 1961 and the end of an era. Would the ghosts of Bader, Ryder, Maughan and the host of pilots that had flown here, some having given their lives, have looked down on the airfield and recalled its glorious past? They were the heroes that ensured RAF Duxford would live in the memory long after its closure.

Spitfire Mark 5 – in Hangar 4

Hawker Hunter with 65 Squadron markings – in Hangar 4

Gloster Meteor – in Hangar 4

German V1 Rocket (Doodle Bug) – in Hangar 4

King's College Chapel – Cambridge

River Cam – Cambridge

An attractive street – Cambridge

A street in historic Stamford

IWM Duxford Airshow September 2012 – Section of the crowd

IWM Duxford Airshow – Display by Red Arrows Aerobatic Team

IWM Duxford Air Show – Spitfire T9 returning from a flying display

IWM Duxford Air Show – Climb aboard a VC10

IWM Duxford Air Show – Antonov Biplane and Dakota on display

IWM Duxford Air Show – Visitors study a plan of the airfield

R.A.F DUXFORD
1920 – CLOSURE

DID YOU SERVE THERE?

OLD DUX ASSOCIATION WELCOMES ANYONE INTERESTED ALL RANKS AND TRADES

VISIT OUR WEBSITE @ http://www.olddux.org/

MEETING BI-ANNUALLY

For details please phone Dartford (01322) 274245 or alternatively write to Mr J.G.Garlinge, 45 Trevithick Drive, Dartford, Kent DA1 5JH

j.f.garlinge@aol.com

Our aims are to reunite old friends and comrades who have lost contact over the years. We hope to provide an opportunity to recapture and experience the spirit of the place and time and the people, to perpetuate the memory

Old Dux Association poster

CHAPTER EIGHT

Duxford Aerodrome Today - Home to the Imperial War Museum Duxford

Today, the Imperial War Museum at Duxford is one of five Museum sites in this country and one of the largest centres for aircraft restoration in the world. It is home to an impressive collection of over 200 aircraft, military vehicles and boats. Established as a vital centre of aviation history it attracts countless visitors, not only to the see the exhibits and observe the important and skilled restoration work at first hand, but also to attend its renowned air displays.

My visit in 2012 to gather material for this book formed an altogether different experience to my earlier one in 1980. To me, the character of the aerodrome had completely changed, although it was none the worse for that. People today will not look back as I did through rose-coloured spectacles at the transformation that had taken place. Duxford had moved on and the Imperial War Museum Duxford had made great strides, presenting not only a fine display of aircraft, both on view and under restoration,but many other attractions.

An example of how things had changed was demonstrated by the impressive modern building incorporating the entrance to the Museum and the visitor centre. Having paid my entrance fee I entered an expansive shop, displaying an infinite variety of books, many of them dealing with the armed forces. Also on display was audio visual material, photographs, educational resources and a wide selection of souvenirs and gifts.

Adjacent to the visitor centre looms the massive Super Hangar (Hangar 1) housing the Airspace exhibition that tells the story of British and Commonwealth aviation since the early days of flight. Its aircraft hall contains more than thirty historic aircraft ranging from the early biplane to Concorde and beyond and it is complemented by the Exhibition Gallery, featuring an interactive experience for all ages and levels of interest.

Routine servicing of the previously mentioned aircraft and the VC10, Avro Vulcan and B52 bomber takes place in the hangar. I was particularly struck by the sight of the Vulcan at close quarters, for I remember it featuring in the 'V Bomber' series, together with the Vickers Valiant and the Handley Page Victor. These three aircraft, revolutionary at the time, comprised Britain's strategic nuclear strike force. In my opinion the Vulcan, with its swept back wings looked the finest of the three. It came into service with the RAF in 1957 at the time of the 'Cold War' when there were concerns about nuclear war. It served as a nuclear weapon carrier for almost all its working life, armed initially with bombs and then, in 1963, with the Blue Steel stand-off missile. In 1982 its cargo was changed to conventional weapons when it was used during the Falklands War to bomb Port Stanley. At that time the Vulcan was nearing the end of its useful life and six aircraft of this type were converted into air-to-air refueling tankers and served from 1982 to 1984.

Another aircraft on display in Airspace is the de Havilland Comet4, that sleek and impressive type of aircraft similar to the Comet 2 that transported some of 65 Squadron ground crew, including me, to Cyprus in 1958. It was part of the fleet operated by British Overseas Airways (BOAC) who launched the world's first passenger jet service in 1952 with the Comet 1. This aircraft cut flying times by half and became extremely popular, but in 1954 a series of serious accidents caused the grounding of all Comet 1's. BOAC began a rigorous investigation into the cause of the disasters, which was found to be stress-related, causing fracture of the fuselage.

I have often wondered what happened to the Comet 2 that I left at Nicosia airport with a hole in its fuselage. I imagine it was repaired and put back into service. However, it was soon superseded by the Comet 3 that was of improved design and construction. This later model carried more passengers and had a longer range. Due to the problems concerning the Comet 1, the Comet 3 programme was abandoned and the Comet 3 frame was used to develop the impressive Comet 4.

The Comet was definitely a pioneering machine, for in addition to being the world's first passenger jet, two of them, one westbound and another eastbound, made the first jet-powered passenger flights across the Atlantic in 1958.

The one making the record-setting eastbound trans-Atlantic

flight is on view in Airspace.

If you thought the Imperial War Museum Duxford was purely about aircraft, I discovered a multitude of additional activities and displays during my visit. For example the Airspace Conference Centre has a range of exclusive suites and rooms accommodating a variety of events. There is even a 200 capacity lecture theatre and corporate facilities. Evening events are available, such as, up to 800 visitors dining in style beneath the wings of Concorde, or dancing the night away USAAF style in another exhibition building, the American Air Museum.

Beyond the Airspace building I found four large hangars, three of which date from 1918. These have been restored and would have been on site during my time there. Within the first of these, the modern Hanger 2, entitled Flying Aircraft, you will find privately-owned historic aeroplanes and the facilities for their restoration, maintenance and preparation for flight. Aircraft, such as the Spitfire, Hurricane and American Mustang, can not only be viewed throughout the year, but take to the air during flying displays demonstrating Duxford's role as a wartime base.

Several naval and maritime aircraft are also exhibited and have exotic names such as Hellcat, Bearcat and Wildcat. A rather unusual-looking American aircraft, the Catalina, is also on view and has its twin engines mounted almost above the cockpit. Air shows are staged regularly with many of the aircraft on show taking part in these varied and entertaining displays.

A piece of Duxford's hidden history has recently been discovered in front of Hangar 2. It concerns a scarab beetle etched into the ground. The previous hangar on this site was used by 64 Squadron, whose badge contains such a beetle, which refers to the 1930's when the Squadron was based temporarily in Egypt. 64 Squadron was the sister squadron to 65 Squadron during my time at Duxford, flying Gloster Javelins.

Some privately-owned aircraft based at Duxford are in regular demand for air displays and filming work. One of the most famous of these aeroplanes, the B17 Flying Fortress *Sally B* is on display in Hangar 2. It is the star of the film *Memphis Belle* that was shot at the airfield in 1989. During filming the airfield became home to five B17 Flying Fortresses, seven Mustang fighters and three Messerschmitt109's.

In Hangar 3 I found an exhibition entitled Air and Sea, which demonstrates how aircraft, boats and vehicles have undergone development from the early days to the present. Exhibits included Coastal Motorboats and Motor Torpedo boats. The former were developed for the Royal Navy during World War One. They were designed to attack large ships with torpedoes and operated mainly off the Dutch and Belgian coast. After World War One several of these craft were helping White Russian forces during the Russian Civil War that followed the 1917 revolution. Lieutenant Augustus Agar R.N. was in command of two of this type of craft and used them on undercover perilous missions, ferrying spies into enemy territory. In 1919 he carried out an audacious attack on the Russian cruiser, *Oleg*. For this feat he was awarded the Victoria Cross.

Motor Torpedo Boats were used in the Second World War to creep into the enemy fleet, carry out an attack and make a quick getaway, or to combat their German counterparts in British coastal waters. These enemy surface ships, such as E-boats posed a threat to British vessels in those waters.

The X-craft exhibition in Air and Sea illustrates the development and use of midget submarines that were designed to attack particular naval targets in problematic waters. The most memorable of such attacks took place in a Norwegian Fjord in 1943 when six X-craft attacked the German battleship *Tirpitz*. It was one of the resounding successes of the Second World War that raised the spirits of the nation. The *Tirpitz* was initially utilised as the centerpiece of the German Baltic Fleet, which was intended to prevent a possible breakout attempt by the Soviet Baltic Fleet. In early 1942 the battleship sailed to Norway to act as a deterrent against Allied invasion and it tried twice to intercept Allied convoys to the Soviet Union. Both attempts failed, but, despite its inability to attack convoys directly its presence forced the Royal Navy to keep significant naval forces in the area to contain it. In September 1943, together with the battleship *Sharnhorst*, the *Tirpitz* bombarded Allied positions on the island of Spitzbergen in the Arctic Circle.

Shortly afterwards, *Tirpitz* came under attack from the six X-craft that damaged the battleship and subsequently it was subjected to a series oflarge-scale air raids. It was finally destroyed by Lancaster bombers that recorded two direct hits, causing *Tirpitz* to capsize.

As I looked around the interior of an X-craft on display I sympathised with its crew who must have suffered very cramped and claustrophobic conditions. Many people remember the flamboyant and brave actions of RAF pilots during the two World Wars, but to me the confined spaces of the X-craft demonstrated the unsung and appalling conditions suffered by countless unglamorous servicemen that served their country during those conflicts.

Air and Sea also displays maritime aircraft operated by members of the Fleet Air Arm that played their part in the defence of Britain. Two aircraft that were at the forefront of operations during the Suez campaign were the Sea Hawk and Sea Vixen at a time when jet planes were being used in conjunction with aircraft carriers. This operation required the adoption of techniques for rapid take-off and landing, of which steam-powered catapults were one feature. The Sea Hawk was particularly useful thanks to its manoeuvrability and ease of control. Five squadrons were deployed on aircraft carriers, able to strike at targets well beyond the reach of land-based aircraft. After the Sea Hawks were retired from front line service by the Fleet Air Arm in 1960 many were used by the navies of West Germany, India and the Netherlands.

The helicopter became an important weapon in later years and the Westland Wasp version, on view in Air and Sea, began its service in 1964 and lasted until 1986 before its retirement, having been part of the Falklands Task Force. Other Wasps, on board HMS *Endurance*, attacked an Argentine submarine during that conflict just prior to South Georgia being recaptured by the British in 1982. The Wasp proved a popular aircraft due to its compactness, its light weight and its ability to operate from a small hangar and flight deck on board anti-submarine frigates and patrol ships.

Hangar 4 houses the Battle of Britain exhibition plus a variety of aircraft associated with the air defence of Great

Britain, ranging from the World War One Bristol Fighter to the McDonnell Douglas Phantom and aircraft used during the Cold War. I was mentally transferred back to my time at Duxford, for I recognised many of the aircraft on display as I gazed nostalgically at the well-maintained Hunter, Javelin and Meteor, aircraft I had come to know and respect during my service. The Spitfire seemed to be the main attraction for my fellow visitors of all ages. It is still a very evocative aeroplane, probably through its reputation during the Battle of Britain and its attraction has never waned. This is strange, for the Hurricane, also on view, was the main British fighter taking part in the Battle of Britain and it seems to play second-fiddle to the Spitfire. Thirty-two RAF squadrons flew Hurricanes at that time along with only nineteen squadrons equipped with Spitfires. In 1940 the Hurricane destroyed more enemy aircraft than all the other aircraft combined. The Hurricane on display was recovered from a crash site in Russia.

There are not only British aircraft in the hangar. Germany was represented by the Messerschmitt 109, its most famous fighter of the Second World War. The one on display was involved in combat in the Battle of France and the Battle of Britain and it destroyed five Allied aircraft in those confrontations. It did not survive the Second World War, for it suffered engine failure in September 1940 and crash-landed in a field near East Dean in Sussex. Its pilot was wounded and taken into captivity. By 1940 the Luftwaffe had over 1,000 of these accomplished fighters in its ranks and their performance exceeded that of the RAF's Hurricane and was only equalled by the Spitfire.

First World War aircraft were represented by the Bristol F2B Fighter, which is a two-seater biplane that became the most successful Allied aircraft on the Western Front during 1917-1918. It remained in service for a period after that war and was used as late as 1931by the University Air Squadron at Duxford. The Bristol on show appeared in splendid condition and its distinctive large orange propeller was conspicuous, which added a touch of class to the well-preserved machine.

Alongside the Gloster Meteor stands a V1 German rocket, given the nickname of 'doodlebug,' used towards the end of the Second World War. The weapon resembles a gigantic cigar with an engine mounted above its tailplane. People living in and around London, its main target area, used to listen for the sound of its engine during a raid, for when it stopped the missile would plummet to earth. The Meteor was the only Allied jet aircraft in service during the Second World War and it achieved some success against the V1's in 1944.

I could not resist having a close look at the gleaming Hawker Hunter on display. It was attached to 65 Squadron at Duxford and in all probability I had worked on it during my service. The squadron emblem was another memory-jerker. Proudly displayed on the aircraft's fuselage, it consists of fifteen chevrons depicting the number of aircraft shot down by the squadron at the climax of the Battle of Britain. The caption on the display board adjacent to the aeroplane indicates that the Hunter was probably the most successful British post-war combat aircraft and also the standard RAF fighter of the 1950's. It also shows that this particular aircraft joined 65 Squadron at RAF Duxford in 1956 and it remained with the unit until 1961 when the station was closed.

Anti-aircraft guns including the Bofors gun were represented and a variant of a Bloodhound missile, designed to shoot down enemy bombers, completed the exhibition.

The next hangar (Hangar 5) is described as Conservation in Action. Within, a team of dedicated staff and volunteers conserve and restore the numerous aircraft and other exhibits of the Imperial War Museum Duxford. They carry out their skilled work often under the scrutiny of the many visitors, during which time they remedy the effects of decay and corrosion and endeavour to prevent future deterioration of the exhibits. Many of the materials used in aircraft construction are at risk of deterioration and must be handled and applied with extreme care. The work in progress that I observed varied from complete dismantling to cleaning and painting.

I learned that the aircraft must be kept in the correct environmental conditions. Fluctuating heat, high humidity and even vigorous cleaning can result in serious damage. Some of the work undertaken involves radical rebuilding of the exhibits. They are gathered from all parts of the globe and sometimes have been in storage outside for several years and require major remedial work. An example is a partially intact aircraft that was still on the production line when that particular project was cancelled and therefore had many of its parts missing. All the existing paint was stripped off when the aircraft was brought into the hangar to reveal the extent of corrosion. The corrosion damage was repaired and then missing panels had to be manufactured, replicating as close to the original material as possible. To complete the renovation the aircraft was repainted in its original colours with accurate stencils and markings.

Current restorations also include a Heinkel HE 111, an Airspeed Ambassador and a de-Havilland Vampire. The German Heinkel, a medium bomber, provided invaluable support to German troops during the 'Blitzkrieg' despite being originally designed as a civilian airliner for Lufthansa. Its military potential was so great that it was modified and bore the brunt of the fighting during the early stages of the Second World War. Unfortunately, its vulnerability to British Fighters resulted in its transfer to night operations.

The Airspeed Ambassador is the sole survivor of twenty-three built for BEA (British European Airways) and operated between 1952 and 1958. It was purchased by the Jordanian Air Force in 1960 until being bought by Dan-Air to carry passengers and freight. In September 1971 it flew from Jersey to Gatwick, the last scheduled flight by an Ambassador. This type of aircraft is particularly remembered for the Munich Disaster when it crashed during take-off with the Manchester United team on board.

The last of the trio, the de-Havilland Vampire I had met before at RAF Tangmere and recalled the screaming noise of its engine. It was the second jet fighter to enter service with the RAF, but unfortunately arrived too late to feature in World War Two. It served with front line squadrons until 1955 and was used for training purposes until 1966. During its life-span this versatile aircraft was attached to many air forces around the world, setting several aviation records, including being the first RAF fighter to exceed 500 miles per hour. In 1945 the Sea Vampire, its naval equivalent, became the first jet aircraft to take off and land on an aircraft carrier and in 1948 it was the first jet plane to fly across the Atlantic.

I always considered this aircraft to be of unusual shape and it seems I was not alone, for its original name was 'Spider Crab,' and many of its design features were developed from the de-Havilland Swallow DH 108. Geoffrey de-Havilland, the company's chief test pilot and son of its founder, flew the prototype on its maiden flight.

Adjacent to Hangar 4 stands a building that is well worth a visit. It is a recreation of Duxford's original 'Op's Room,' from where RAF pilots were guided into combat during the Battle of Britain. You will recall the enlivening duet between 'Woodie' (Wing Commander Woodhall) and 'Dogsbody' (Wing Commander Douglas Bader) in Chapter 7 that was performed during sorties from Duxford. They provided some light relief during chastening periods of combat when 'Woodie' did a fine job as Op's Controller.

The building housing the American Air Museum is 'state-of-the-art' and it was designed by no less than the renowned architect Lord (Norman) Foster. It is intended as a tribute and memorial to the thousands of United States airmen who lost their lives while flying from British bases. The exhibition within illustrates the history of American air power and its effect on the two World Wars, with a fine collection of combat aircraft that have been utilised over the years. A large number of exhibits are suspended from the roof in an appropriate flying configuration to give a touch of realism to the display.

Military aviation was outperformed by its civil counterpart between the two World Wars, but by 1945 the balance was redressed and US air power was undeniable. Towards the end of the Second World War the US Air Force occupied over 120 British airfields and made a decisive impact on the course of the war in Europe. The US 8th Air Force combined with RAF Bomber Command in an offensive designed to halt Germany's war effort and the 9th Air Force provided support for Allied Forces on the ground.

When The 8th Air Force was at its strongest in 1944, 300 aircraft were being constructed every day by American factories, in fact a total of 325,000 aircraft were built during the conflict. The 8th Air Force flew Boeing B17 Flying Fortresses and B24 Liberator heavy bombers on daylight raids over Germany and occupied Europe. 20,000 airmen in 3,000 bombers with supporting fighters could be utilised in a single day.

To highlight some of the most well-known American aircraft on show in the American Air Museum, I have picked a sample that caught my eye. Firstly, the Flying Fortress, which is probably the most widely recognized American bomber of the Second World War. Initially they flew in massive defensive formations, but were vulnerable to German fighter attacks until better protection was afforded by the long-range P51 Mustangs that could fly with the bombers the whole distance to their targets.

The Flying Fortress in the exhibition was rebuilt and repainted to represent the *Mary Alice*, an aircraft of that type that flew around ninety-eight combat missions. A later version is also on show, the long-range B29 Superfortress, with a partly-pressurised fuselage and remote controlled gun turrets. It was the most advanced bomber of the Second World War and it was used in the strategic bombing of Japan. In the early days of the Cold War the plane was the main US Air Force nuclear deterrent and the one on display flew bombing raids during the Korean War.

The B24 Liberator bomber on view has the name 'Dugan' on its fuselage, superimposed with an emblem that resembles a clover leaf.

What of the bombers' fighter protection? Their main escort fighter during 1943 and early 1944 was the P47 Thunderbolt that has been referred to for its limited range. To overcome this deficiency drop tanks were utilised, but were not fully successful and the aircraft was phased out and replaced by the P51 Mustang, which could also operate as a fighter-bomber. However, the durable P47 was then used in a ground attack capacity with the 9th Air Force. Duxford's P47 displays the markings of Colonel Zemke's *Oregon's Britannia* and is named after the illustrious commander of the top-scoring 56th Fighter Group. Colonel Hubert Zemke, known 'Hud' to his fellow servicemen, was a leading USAAF ace pilot and the '56th' was given the nickname of 'Zemke's Wolf Pack,' being the first to fly the P47 Thunderbolt fighter.

In 1940 Zemke was sent to England as a combat observer with the RAF, studying their tactics and those of the Luftwaffe; observations he would use later when the United States entered World War Two. Initially, he was on temporary assignment testing the new P47 Thunderbolt, before being sent to England with the 56th Fighter Group in January 1943 to escort bombers over Europe. In June of that year he scored his first two kills and during October the 'Wolf Pack's' score was 39 enemy aircraft destroyed for only one of theirs.

Zemke became a master tactician, utilising the P47's best qualities and initiated the mantra, 'dive, fire and recover.' He was an important figure in turning the tide of the war by developing tactics that allowed U.S. fighters to break from close escort to attack enemy fighters before they could get to their bombers. These tactics were adopted in a modified form by all Groups of the 8th Air Force in early 1945 and other innovations made the P47 a superior aerial weapon.

Under Zemke's command the 56th claimed over 500 German aircraft destroyed, of which Zemke claimed fifteen and for his achievements he was awarded the DSC (Distinguished Service Cross).

He was then transferred to the 479th Fighter Group where he made one of the first probable kills of a German jet fighter. Whilst leading the 479th he was credited with two and a half aircraft destroyed.

In October 1944 a wing of Zemke's aircraft was torn off whilst flying through severe turbulence. Forced to bail out over enemy territory, Zemke was taken prisoner after several days trying to avoid capture. Whilst he was being transported by train between interrogations, Allied fighters strafed the carriages causing the train to stop. Jumping from the train he was about to flee when he realised that escape was impossible, even in the confusion, due to the surrounding bleak landscape.

Zemke re-boarded the train and pulled two young girls from the line of fire as the fighters made another pass and for this act he was almost awarded a Nazi medal for bravery. For his action in this situation and the respect he earned from his interrogators Zemke became Senior Allied Officer of Stalag Luft 1 at Barth.

He was put in charge of 7,000 Allied prisoners, which grew to 9,000, languishing in terrible conditions. Through his persuasion of the prison Commandant he managed to achieve some improvements to their plight.

When it became apparent that the war was lost the Germans became more cooperative and when the prisoners were ordered to leave the camp Zemke refused, fearing for their safety. Knowing that the Soviets were drawing ever closer he and his staff made an arrangement for the Germans to leave the camp quietly under the cover of darkness and to hand it over to the prisoners. Zemke cultivated friendly relations with the Soviets who arrived shortly afterwards and eventually he arranged for the POW's to be flown to American territory in B17 bombers shortly after VE Day.

During Zemke's combat service he flew 154 missions and attained seventeen and a half victories.

Another distinctive aircraft that caught my eye in the exhibition was the American U2 spy plane that I recalled seeing on the television news during the Cuban Missile Crisis in October 1962. At this time the world was on the brink of nuclear war and the U2 spy planes were being used for reconnaissance over the Soviet Union. Unfortunately, one such aircraft was shot down and its pilot taken prisoner, causing an international incident. However, sorties by U2s were also flown closer to home and they revealed that Soviet medium-range missiles were being installed on the Caribbean island of Cuba, on America's doorstep. President John F. Kennedy demanded their removal and US forces were placed on full alert, with nuclear bombers being put on continuous airborne patrols. Thankfully, the Russians backed down and removed their missiles. Grateful for this move, the US removed missiles from Turkey and one of the most dramatic incidents of the Cold War was defused.

The final building on my tour was entitled Land Warfare, which demonstrates how ground combat has changed over the years and the mechanisation of warfare has altered the way in which battles are fought. From the great artillery barrages of the First World War, through the widespread tank battles of the Second World War, to the highly mechanised clashes of today, the exhibition within Land Warfare shows the nature of this change. Some of the vehicles and equipment involved are as follows:

The American 3-ton General Service truck was used by the Allies from 1915 onwards, remaining in use until 1930. On the Western Front theses vehicles were in universal use for towing large artillery weapons, as repair shops, balloon winches and searchlight trucks. They proved their worth and by 1918 the Allies had 3,000 of this type of vehicle in use. Also on show is the British Heavy Howitzer, used during the First World War. It had seen service during the Boer War and was capable of firing six-inch shells that could wreak considerable damage on the enemy.

A German tank, the Panzer IV was used as the main battle tank on all their fronts during the Second World War. It was utilised in the invasion of Poland, France, Russia and the Balkans during the 'Blitzkrieg' offensive as part of the Panzer Divisions. Following airborne attack on the enemy, often by Stuka dive-bombers, the tanks would break through enemy lines at a pre-planned point speedily followed by supporting artillery and mobile troops.

The Panzer IV is one amongst several on display, which include the Canadian version of the American Sherman tank and the Soviet T/34 medium tank. The latter was recognised in many quarters as the best designed tank of its era and provided the most serious challenge to the German armies during World War Two. It was so successful it remained in use after the war and some are still operating around the world today. A tank of later vintage, the Centurion, was used by the British during the Korean War (1951-1953) and proved a highly successful weapon. The one on display came into use in 1942 and became a training vehicle in the late 1950's.

In 1991 the British Army fought in the Gulf War as part of a United Nations Force and used the Challenger tank that is included in the exhibition along with one of the more unusual items of hardware known as the 'Wheelbarrow.' This is a remotely-operated bomb-disposal machine, capable of several functions including a remote-controlled pick-up device and X-ray equipment.

Of particular interest are the Montgomery Caravans, the three-vehicle mobile headquarters used by Field Marshal Montgomery in the African and north-west Europe campaigns. The first caravan was seized from the Italians in 1942 and became his home for the following nine months until a second caravan was captured. 'Monty,' as he was affectionately known, transformed the first caravan into his bedroom and used the second as his office. He also acquired a lorry that became his tactical headquarters after D-Day in June 1944 and, together with his other two vehicles, it was utilised until the German surrender in May 1945. During that period he received a visit from King George VI to his headquarters and gave his majesty a briefing on the progress of the war in Europe.

An additional item of interest to the various exhibitions is the commercial aircraft on display near Hangars 4 and 5. On the South-West Apron stand the Hawker Siddley Trident, Bristol Britannia and the Handley Page Dart Herald.

Near the American Air Museum you will find a McDonnell Douglas F15, a twin-engined all weather American tactical fighter, considered to be among the most successful modern fighters with over 100 aerial victories and no losses in dogfights. The plane served with the USAAF from 1972 until around 2005. It can climb to 30,000 feet in approximately sixty seconds and its thrust is such it can take off almost vertically.

If you are not content with looking at or around aircraft and desire the thrill of being airborne there are flights available on the light planes to be found parked on the grass near the South-West Apron. You have a choice between a Dragon Rapide, Tiger Moth or AT16 Harvard that will provide a bird's eye view of the airfield as well as the surrounding countryside.

Between hangars 3 and 4 a Bloodhound S.A.M. missile can be seen pointing its nose skywards. This surface to air missile was developed during the 1950's as Britain's main defensive weapon. It was widely used by the RAF and the forces of four other countries after its inception in 1958.

(Whilst every effort has been made for accuracy, it should be stressed that the type of aircraft and equipment on view can be changed, as can their location).

Near the main entrance, as though on guard duty and welcoming visitors to the Museum is a Hurricane fighter perched on a pole, a lasting reminder of the part played by RAF Duxford during the dark days of the Second World War.

Afterword

Since completing my National Service I have discovered that a number of men who should have served for two years in the forces managed to escape call-up. Apparently, the easiest way to avoid conscription was to ignore the summons to register for National Service. Thanks to a shortage of staff at that time to enforce attendance, this method of avoidance was very effective.

Another method was to hire a man who had failed his medical to impersonate you before the Medical Board. One such person was rejected as unfit for service due to an enlarged heart and found that he could make money in this way. Unfortunately, for him, he was arrested and charged with impersonating eight different men at various Medical Boards. It was revealed during his court appearance that one man had paid him several thousand pounds for his services.

A further lucrative opportunity for cheats was the sale of forged medical discharge certificates and at one time the police in London were investigating several gangs reputed to be selling these certificates. Unscrupulous doctors were willing to issue false medical certificates to relatives, friends, or those wishing to avoid conscription. An investigation by the General Medical Council resulted in some of these doctors being struck off and one doctor was found to have 700 forged certificates in his possession when he was arrested.

When summoned to appear before the Medical Board I was so young and innocent that it never crossed my mind to take advantage of such schemes.

I also learned that some unfortunate recruits had to serve for two and a half years – an extra six months – due to conflicts taking place in various countries, such as the advent of the 'Cold War,' the Malayan Emergency, Suez, Aden and the Korean War. These resulted in insufficient regulars being available and National Servicemen were required to fill the gap.

A great deal was written, or portrayed on television about National Service being two years of inactivity and boredom, which has upset some relatives of National Servicemen, for thousands of them lost their lives or became casualties in the various campaigns. The last intake of National Servicemen took place in 1960 and a crisis relating to the erection of the Berlin Wall delayed the end of conscription for these unfortunates.

Some National Servicemen were persuaded to 'sign on' and become regulars, as the opportunity for travel, to learn new skills and forge new careers presented themselves. However, the other side of the coin was that in some respects the armed forces did not exploit the skills and knowledge gained by recruits as a civilian. For example, a friend was obliged to sit an officer selection test during his induction into the RAF as a National Serviceman, thanks to his having attended Grammar School. He did well in the examination – finishing seventh - but was unsuccessful in gaining a commission, mainly due to his family background. He and the remainder of the top forty candidates were randomly posted to the RAF Regiment, the fighting arm of that service and he spent the majority of his two years' service in Iraq as a signaller.

Where a man was posted was the luck of the draw. Even if one had requested 'any country abroad,' the likelihood was he would get a home posting and conversely, if a home posting was asked for he would probably be sent abroad. The latter happened to two fellow recruits who were both married and requested to stay in this country. They were both sent to trouble spots abroad. The only consolation for them was the extra pay for married men and a duty-free existence. One recruit, who had not asked for a particular posting, was not even allowed to finish basic training before being told, 'You are going tomorrow.' For one glorious moment the man thought it meant he was going home, but he was posted abroad and was probably the only recruit that never took part in a 'passing out' parade.

To update you with progress on the National Citizen Service, the latest figure available at the time of writing– during 2011, 8,500 young people took advantage of the scheme and participated in its three weeks of team-building, outdoor activities and the opportunity to meet like-minded people from all walks of life and the chance to make a difference to their community. Working in teams enabled them to bond with each other by taking part in such activities as mountaineering, canoeing and abseiling. They also had the opportunity to design and deliver a chosen project within their own communities, which meant working with other young people to improve the area in which they live. The aim was to improve the life of their community and help it to appreciate what can be achieved by working together. Although the scheme does not involve the strict discipline and demands of military training it fostered a feeling of achievement in tackling new challenges.

In 2012 the National Citizen Service Partnership has provided places for over 26,000 young people to take part during the summer in the second year of the Government's national pilot scheme. Twenty-nine providers ran National Citizen Service schemes for around 21,000 young people.

In 2013, 30,000 places are to be made available and previously the National Citizen Service has only operated in the summer holidays, but following the success of the programme the Government is looking at ways to offer it all year round for 16 and 17-year-olds.

In 2014 the number of participants is expected to rise to 90,000. I wish the scheme every success.

Index

A White Sports Coat and a Pink Carnation 16
Aden 68
Aeroplane and Armament Experimental Establishment 57
Afghanistan Conflict 62
Agar, Augustus, Lieutenant R.N. 137
Air and Sea (Hangar3) 137, 138
Aircraftsman Hunt 38, 39, 40
Air Day (1975) 131, 132
Air Ministry 50, 87, 100
Airspace (Hangar1)135, 136
Airspace Conference Centre 135
Airspeed Ambassador 141
Alexandria 77
Alfie 41
All I Have to do is Dream 71
Alps, the 69
America 83
American Air Museum 136, 143, 147
American Independence Day 45
American Midwest 84
Amman 67
Anson, George, Admiral 61
Arc de Triomphe 89
'Arch to Arc' Race 89
Armstrong Whitworth Siskin 98
Arsenal F.C. 81
Arts Council 28
Arundel 42
Aswan Dam 52
Atlantic Ocean 142
Avro 504 98
Avro Anson 61, 62
Avro Lancaster 22
Avro Tutor 101
Avro Vulcan 134

B 52 Bomber 134
Bader, Douglas, Group Captain 45, 48, 73, 98, 99, 100, 101, 102, 103,104, 105, 106, 107, 108, 109, 110,111, 112, 113, 114, 115, 116, 117,118, 119, 120, 121, 122, 123, 124,126, 127,133, 142
Baghdad Revolution 67
Barth 144
Basildon 94
Bass, Alfie 83

Battle of Britain 36, 44, 45, 46, 61, 84, 85, 87, 98, 99, 103, 104, 110, 112, 129, 139, 140, 142,
Battle of Britain 88, 129
'Battle of Britain Day' 108
Battle of Britain Exhibition (Hangar4) 138
Battle of France 46, 103
Battle of the Nile 77
Battle of the Pyramids 77
Bay of Naples 69
BBC Home Service 30
BEA 90, 141
'Bealine Syndicate' 90
Bedford, Brian 94
Bedfordshire 3
Beirut 68
Bell P-39 Airacobra 127
Bentley Priory 44
Berlin 119, 123
Berlin Airlift 75
Black Arrows, the 60
Black September 67
Blackburn Beverley 66, 68
Blackpool 25, 27, 30
Blackpool Grand Theatre 28, 30
Blackpool Grand Theatre Trust 28
Blackpool Tower 28
Blackpool Tower Ballroom 28
Blackpool Tower Company 28
Blackpool Winter Gardens 28
Bleriot, Louis 89
Bletchley Park 49
Blitz, the 112
'Blitzkrieg' 141
Blue Steel Missile 135
Boer War 146
BOAC 135
BoforsGun 140
Bofors Site 105
Bolton Wanderers F.C. 82
Bond, James 41
Boone, Pat 17
Bootham, Flight Lieutenant 51
Bootsy and Snudge 83
Boscombe Down 57
Breslau 119
Bresslaw, Bernard 83
Brian and Margaret 94
Brickhlill, Paul 106
Bridewell Museum 63
Bridgnorth 6, 19, 21, 22, 24

Bridgnorth Town Council 23
Bridgnorth Veterans 23
Bristol Blenheim 53, 99
Bristol Britannia 147
Bristol Fighter 98, 139
Britain 49, 50, 52, 53, 67, 68, 72,73, 76, 83, 98, 103, 138
British Army 146
British Commonwealth 103
British Empire 4, 78, 103
British Expeditionary Force (BEF) 102, 130
British Heavy Howitzer 146
Brooke, Sir Alan, General 63
Brussels 117, 118
Buckinghamshire 49
Burma 53
Burns, Jim, Flight Lieutenant 89
Busby Babes 81
Busby, Sir Matt 81, 82
Byrne, Roger 82

Cagney, James 128
Caine, Michael 41
Cambridge 55, 94, 95
Cambridge Guildhall 128
Cambridgeshire 104, 112
Cambridge University Air Squadron 98
Camm, Sir Sydney 38
Canary Islands 78
Canterbury 109
Cape Wrath 124
Carravaggio 77
Carry On Films 83
Carson Sisters 30
Carson, Violet 30
Catalina (Flying Boat) 136
Central Fighter Establishment 49
Central Flying School 101
Central London 89
Centurian Tank 146
Challenger Tank 146
Chamberlin, Neville 63, 99
Channel, (English) 47, 76, 86, 89,109, 113, 128
Charlie's Aunt 28
Charlton, Bobby 82
Chelsea 89
Chelsea Embankment 89
Cheshire 25
Chichester 35, 36, 37, 41, 45

Children's Hour 30
Chinook Helicopter 62
Churchill, Lady 73
Churchill, Winston 44, 46, 48,72, 73, 103,111
Churchill's Secret Army 49
Coastal Motorboats 137
Cochran, Eddie 84.
'Cold War' 52, 135, 139, 145
Colditz Castle 121, 122, 123
Colman, Eddie 82
Como, Perry 16
Concorde 132, 133, 134, 136
Conservation in Action140
Coote, Patrick 99
Corbett, Ronnie 23
Coronation Street 30
Coward, Jimmie, Flight Lieutenant 112, 113
Cowes 50
Cuba 145
Cuban Missile Crisis 145
Curtiss P-40's 47
Curtiss P-40 Kittyhawk 46
Curtiss P-40 Tomahawk 46
Cyprus 6, 52, 56, 66, 67, 68, 72, 73, 75, 82, 94
Cyprus Mail 84
Czechoslovakia 85

D-Day 127, 147
D-Day Landings 62
Dacey (Drill Instructor) 13
Dalton, Hugh 48
Dan-Air 141
Day, Harry 119
deHavilland Comet 68, 73, 75,90, 135
deHavilland Comet Sabotage 74
deHavilland, Geoffrey 142
deHavilland Swallow 142
de Havilland Vampire 22, 29, 40,59, 62, 88, 141
deHavilland Venom 88
Department of the Environment132
Derbyshire 25
Dodd, Ken 30
Domino, Fats 84
Donaldson E.M. GroupCaptain49,
Dornier 46, 85, 102, 104, 105,107, 109, 112
Dover 111, 116
Dowding, Hugh, Air Marshal 44

Drake, Billy, Group Captain 46
Dragon Rapide 147
Drumrunie 126
Duke, Neville, Squadron Leader49
DulagLuft 118
Dundas, 'Cocky' 113
Dunkirk 88, 102
Durness 124, 126
Duxford Aerodrome 101
Duxford Airfield 98, 132
Duxford Aviation Society 132

E-Boats 137
East Anglian Aviation Society
132
East Dean 139
Eden, Anthony 52, 53
Edinburgh 65
Edward IV 95
Edward, Duke of York 95
Edwards, Duncan 81, 82
Edwards, Thelma 100, 103, 115,
118, 123
Egypt 47, 52, 53, 76, 136
El Gamil 75
Elizabeth II 62
Elphin 126
Emery, Dick 83
England 22, 28, 34, 45, 46, 48,83,
115,144
English Heritage 28
EOKA 56, 67, 69, 72
EOKA Campaign 56
Eton College 95
Europe 101, 127, 133, 143, 144
Everly Brothers 71,

F.A. Cup Final 92
Fairey Battle 101
Falklands Task Force 138
Falklands War 135
Famagusta 69
Farnborough Air Show 60, 61,71
Farnborough Airfield 70
Fife 65
Fisher, George 34, 35
Fiske, Billy 45
Fisz, Benjamin 129
Fleet Air Arm 44, 88, 138
Flying Fortress, B17, *Sally B* 136,
Flying Fortress, B17, *Mary Alice*143
Flying Aircraft (Hangar 2) 136

Flying Training School (no.2) 62,98
Fort Leavenworth 48
Fort St. Almo 78
Fort St. Angelo 78
Foster, Norman, Lord 142
France 4, 22, 46, 52, 53, 63, 87,102, 110,
112, 131, 146
Frankfurt 117
Fraser, Bill 83
Freetown 47
Friends of the Grand Theatre,
Blackpool 28, 30
Galland, Adolf 115
Gatwick 141
Geneva Convention 118
George V's Jubilee Review ofthe RoyalAir
Force 98
George VI 22, 45, 76, 127, 130,147
George Cross Island 76
George Cross, the 76
German Baltic Fleet 137
German-Polish Border 120
Germany 98, 116, 117, 127, 139, 143
Gleiwitz 120
Glenn Martin Bomber 47
Gloster IV's 50
Gloster Gamecock 44, 99
Gloster Gauntlet 98, 99
Gloster Gladiators 44
Gloster Grebe 98
Gloster Javelin 56, 57, 59, 129,
136, 139
Gloster Meteor 31, 32, 49, 54, 59, 60,62,
87, 88, 98, 128, 129, 139, 140
Goering, Herman 117
Gosnay 63
Grand Harbour 76, 78
Grantham 79
Gravesend 109, 110
Greece 69
Greek Cypriots 69, 71, 72
Grivas , Colonel 69
Grumman Hellcat 136
Grumman Bearcat 136
Grumman Wildcat 136
Gulf, the 68
Gulf War 146

Halahan, Air Vice Marshal 100
Halifax, Nova Scotia 88
Halton (RAF Hospital) 85
Hamlet 28, 30

Hampshire 61, 62
Handley Page Dart Herald 147
Handley Page Hastings 75, 76, 77, 78
Handley Page Victor 135
Harvard AT16 ?
Have a Go 30
Hawker Demons 84
Hawker Fury 44, 46
Hawker Hinds 53
Hawker Hunter 36, 37, 38, 39, 41, 43, 54, 55, 56, 59, 60, 61, 69, 129, 139, 140, 70, 81, 89, 90, 94
Hawker Hurricane44, 45, 46, 49, 53, 84, 85, 88, 101, 102, 106, 108, 109, 130, 136, 139, 148
Hawker Siddley Trident 147
Hawker Typhoons 48, 62
Hawtrey, Charles 83
Haley, Bill and the Comets
Heinkel 46, 88, 102, 131, 141
Hendon Air Show 100
Henry VI 96
Henry VII 95
Henry VIII 95
Hess, Alexander, 'Sasha,' Squadron Leader 116
High Speed Flight 44, 49, 50
Hindenburgh 4
Hitler, Adolf 22, 99, 106
HMS Endurance 138
Holly, Buddy 83, 84
Hope, Bob 128
Houstan, Lady Lucy 51
Huntingdon 80

Ian and Sheila 91
Imperial Airship Scheme 4
Imperial War Museum (Duxford) 130, 132, 133, 134, 135, 140, 143
Imperial War Museum, (London) 132
India 76, 138
Indonesia 56
Indonesian Confrontation 76
Iraq 67
Israel 52, 53
Italy 49

Japan 48, 53, 143
Jersey 141
Jordan 67
Jordon Crisis 56, 57
Jordanian Air Force 141

Junkers JU87 47
Junkers Stuka

Kenly Wing 98
Kent 109
Kincade, Samuel 50
King Faisal II 67
King Hussain 67
King John 62
Kings College 95
Kings College Chapel 95, 96
Kinloss 35
Kirkham 27
Kirkham Prison 33, 34
Kite Balloons 5
Knight's Hospitaller 76
Korean War 143, 146
Kylesku 126
Kyrenia Mountains 69

Lamsdorf 119, 121
Lancashire 25, 30, 81
Land Warfare 145, 146
Langford, Francis 128
Larnaka 69
Lavington Hole Gardens 24
Laxford Bridge 126
Lebanon 67, 68
Leigh-Mallory, Trafford, Air Vice Marshal 99, 105, 106, 107, 108, 110, 112, 114
Letchworth 65
Letchworth Technical College 64, 65, 66
B24 Liberator 34, 143
Little Richard 84
Littlehampton 49
Liverpool 30, 81
Lockheed Hercules 56
London 37, 91, 107, 109, 110, 111, 112, 123, 140
London Coliseum 28
Londonderry 98
London to Paris Air Race 89
Lubeck 118
Lufthansa 141,
Luftwaffe 44, 62, 87, 103, 107, 115, 131, 139, 144

M 11 Motorway 132
*Mad Passionate Love*83
Magisterial Palace Palace 77
Mahaddie, Hamish, Group Captain 130, 131

Malayan Confrontation 56
Malaysia 56, 76
Malham 91
Malta 46, 47, 75, 76, 78
Maltese Parliament 77
Mamluks, the 77
Manchester 25, 81
Manchester City 81
Manchester United 81, 82
Mansfield 25, 37, 79, 83
B26 Marauder 65
Marble Arch 89
Maronite Christians 68
Marsamxett Harbour 76
Massey, Group Captain 119
Matchum, Frank 28
Maughan, Charles , Squadron Leader 84, 88, 89, 90
McDonnel Douglas F15 147
McDonnel Douglas Phantom 139
Mediterranean 77, 78
Melvin 25, 35
Memphis Belle 136
Messerschmitt (109) 46, 62, 87, 102, 107, 109, 111, 113, 114, 115, 131, 137, 139
Middle East 47, 52, 67, 68, 76
Middlesex 21
Milch, Erhard 62
Miles Master 101
Ministry Of Defence 132
Mitchell, R. J. 51
Montgomery, Bernard, Field Marshal 147
Montgomery Caravans 147
Moray Firth 35
More, Kenneth 88
Mortlock-Donaldson, 'Teddy', Group Captain 49
Motor Torpedo Boats 137
Munich 66
Munich Air Crash 56
Munich Airport 82
Munich Disaster 141
Mustang (P-51) 62, 127, 136

Napoleon Bonaparte 76, 77
National Lottery, the 28
National War Museum 78
Nelson, Horatio 77
Netherlands 138
Newark 79
Nicosia 68, 69, 72, 75, 78

Nieminen, Toni 45
No. 10 School of Technical Training For Airframes and Armament 25
Norman Conquest 63
North Africa 32, 46, 52, 65, 127
North London 108
North Weald 110
Northants 23
Norway 137
Norwich 63
Norwich Cathedral 63
Nottingham 37
Notty Ash 30

O'Connor, Des 23
Odiham 62
Oflag VIB 118
Old Dux Association 95
Olivier, Laurence 3
Operation Sea Lion 103, 111
Order of St. John 76
Ottoman Invasion

Palazzo Parisio 76
Panza IV Tank 146
Paris 89, 90
Paris Air Show 60
Parisot de la Vallette, Jean 76
Pas de Calais 108
Pennine Way 91
'Phoney War' 101
Pickles, Wilfred 30
Pinfold, Herbert, Moreton, Group Captain84, 85, 86, 87, 88
Poland 85, 146
Portland 85
Port Said Governorate 75
Port Stanley 135
Portsmouth 37, 41, 42, 65
Portsmouth Technical College 41
President Eisenhower 53
President Kennedy, John F. 145
President Nasser, Abdul 52
Preston 25, 27, 32, 33, 65
Price, Squadron Leader 111
Princes Street (Edinburgh) 65
Private Popplewell 83

Queen Elizabeth the Queen Mother 83, 127, 130
Quill, Jeffrey 98

R 101 Airship 4
RAF 11 Group 104, 105, 107, 109, 112
RAF 12 Group 104, 105
RAF 12 Group Wing 107, 108, 109, 110, 111, 112, 114, 115, 118
RAF Balloon Training Unit 5
RAF Bassingbourn 132
RAF Biggin Hill 48, 89
RAF Bomber Command 62, 142
RAF Bridgnorth 7, 10, 11, 14, 15, 18, 23, 24, 25, 31, 33, 37, 96
RAF Cardington 3, 4, 5, 6
RAF Coastal Command 62, 68
RAF College, Cranwell 99, 100
RAF Coltishall 102, 104
RAF Cosford 23
RAF Duxford 55, 56, 57, 59, 60, 61, 63, 65, 66, 78, 79, 80, 82, 83, 84, 87, 88, 90, 91, 92, 93, 94, 95, 96, 98, 99, 100, 102, 104, 106, 107, 108, 109, 111, 112, 113, 116, 117, 124, 125, 127, 128, 129, 140, 148
RAF Duxford 'Op's Room 142
RAF Elgin 107
RAF Fighter Command 62, 98, 99, 105
RAF Gambut 47
RAF Halton 23
RAF Hendon 103, 121
RAF Hornchurch 87, 88
RAF Horsham St. Faith 63
RAF Kirkham 25, 30, 32, 33, 34, 37, 39
RAF Kirton-in-Lindsay 102
RAF Krendi 47
RAF Leuchars 33, 65, 66,
RAF Llandow 48
RAF Ludford Magna 107
RAF Museum, Hendon 23
RAF Nicosia 67, 70, 71, 73, 74, 75, 135
RAF North Weald 60, 84
RAF Odiham 61, 62
RAF Staff College 87
RAF Stanmore 21
RAF Swinderby 23
RAF Tangmere 32, 33, 35, 36, 37, 41, 42, 44, 45, 46, 47, 48, 49, 52, 54, 56, 57, 112, 114, 115, 116, 141

RAF Tangmere Wing 53
RAF Tenga 56, 129
RAF Waterbeach 78, 79, 80, 82
Reach for the Sky 106, 126
Red Arrows, the 60
Red Star Belgrade 82
Rhiconich 126
Richard III 95
River Cam 96
River Thames 110
Rock and Roll 84
Rock Around the Clock 84
Rolls Royce 44, 50
Rome 87
Royal Aero Club 52
Royal Air Force 98
Royal Flying Corps 44, 98
Royal Naval Air Service 98
Royal Navy 61, 76, 137
Royal Variety Performance 83
Russia 139, 146
Russian Civil War 137
Ryder, Norman, Group Captain 84, 87, 88, 89, 90, 133
Rylands, Eric 90

St. Andrews 33, 65
St. John's Co-Cathedral 77
St. Omer 63, 115, 118
St. Paul's Cathedral 45
'Sad Sack' Café 34
Saltzman, Harry 129, 130
Schneider, Jacques 49
Schneider Trophy 44, 49, 50, 51, 52
Science Museum 52
Scotland 33, 35
Sea Hawk (Royal Navy) 138
Sea Vampire (Royal Navy) 141
Sea Vixen (Royal Navy) 132, 138
Seawards Homes 55
Sergenson, Thomas 28
Seven Years War 61
Shakespeare, William 28
Sharnhorst 137
Sharples, Ena 30
Sherman Tank 146
Sherborne 85
Short Brothers 4
Short Crusader 50
Shropshire 6

Sierra Leone 47
Sinai Peninsular52
Singapore 48, 53
Solent, the 52
Somerset 85
Sopwith Snipe 98
South Georgia 138
Soviet Baltic Fleet 137
Special Operations Executive
(SOE) 48, 49
'Spider Crab' (Vampire) 142
Spitfire Fund 88
Spitfire Productions 129
Spitzbergen 137
1 Squadron 52
18 Squadron 73
19 Squadron 63, 98, 99,
102, 107
23 Squadron 99
34 Squadron 36, 37, 53
41 Squadron 87, 88
43 Squadron 44
56 Squadron 84, 87
60 Squadron 129
64 Squadron 56, 59, 84, 93, 95,
129, 136
65 Squadron 47, 55, 56, 59, 60,
61, 66,70, 81, 88, 89, 90, 91,
92, 93, 95, 129, 136, 140
66 Squadron 63, 99
111 Squadron 60
112 Squadron 47
128 Squadron 47
213 Squadron 47
222 Squadron 102
242 Squadron 102, 104, 105,
106, 107, 112,
263 Squadron 88
302 Squadron 108
310 Squadron 107, 109
611 Squadron 108
616 Squadron 69
Soviet T/34 Tank 146
Soviet Union 145
Stainforth, Flight Lieutenant 51
StalagLuft I 144
StalagLuft III 119
Stalag VIIIB 119
Stamford 79
Stanmore 21, 23
Stanmore Country Park 21
Stephenson, Geoffrey 121, 122

Straits of Tiran 52
Strath Kinnaird 124, 125, 126
Strangers Hall 63
'Stringbag' Swordfish 88
Stuka (Dive Bomber) 146
Subba Row, Ramon 23
Suez Canal 52
Suez Crisis 44, 52, 75
B29 Superfortress 143
Supermarine S.5 50
Supermarine S.6 51
SupermarineSeafire 88
Supermarine Spitfire 22, 44, 46,
47,51, 62, 63, 84, 88, 98, 102,
107, 109,112, 113, 114, 127,
128, 130, 136, 139
Super Hangar (Hangar1) 134
Supreme Headquarters, Allied
Expeditionary Force48
Sussex 35, 139
Sutherland 124, 126
Swinburne, Algernon, Charles
123
Switzerland 48

Tangier 32
Tangmere Airfield 40, 49
Tangmere Airfield Nurseries 54
Tangmere Cottage 49
Taylor, Tommy 81, 82
Thatcher, Margaret 79
*The Army Game*83
The Backs 95, 96
The Battle of Britain 98
Thunderbolt (P47) 53, 127,
128, 143, 144
Tiger Moth 147
Tipu Sultan 76
Tirpitz 167, 138
Tottenham Hotspur 81
Tower of London 95
Treaty of Paris 62
Tuck, Bob 119
Turky 75, 145
Turkish Cypriots 69
Turkish Invasion 75
Turkish Resistance
Organisation 69
Twelfth Night 30
Twitty, Conway 84

U2 (spy plane) 145

U boat (German) 62
Ullapool 124
United Artists 130, 131
United Nations 53
United Nations Peace-Keeping
Force 75
United States 45, 46, 48, 67,
68, 144
United States Army Air Forces
44, 63
United States Second Tactical
Air Force 48
Upavon 101, 102
USAAF 147
USAAF Duxford 130
U.S. 8th Air Force 127, 142, 144
U.S. 9th Air Force 143
U.S. 12th Air Force 127
U.S. 56th Fighter Group 143, 144
U.S. 78th Fighter Group 127, 128
U.S. 479th Fighter Group 144

V1 German Rocket 139, 140
Valetta 76, 77, 78
Venice 50
Vickers VC10 134
Vickers Valiant 135
Viollet, Dennis 81

Wales 34
Washbrook, Cyril 23
Warburg 118
Wars of the Roses 95
Watford 81
Western Front 139, 146
Wester Ross 124

West Africa 46, 47
West Germany 138
West Suffolk Constabulary 105
Western Alliance 53
Westhampnet 138
Westland Wasp 138
Whittle, Frank 98
Williams, Peter 23
Winchester 62
Windsor 62
Winter Olympics (1936) 45
Wissant 115
Withers, Mr. and Mrs. 34, 35
Whittlesford 105
Woodhall, 'Woodie' Wing
Commander 111, 112, 125, 142
Woodley Airfield 99
World War One 44, 45, 53, 137,
145, 146
World War Two 22, 23, 25, 34,
37, 44, 45, 48, 53, 54, 59, 61,
62,76, 80, 84, 88, 96, 98, 99, 128,
139, 140, 141, 142, 143, 144,
145, 146, 148
Worthing 42, 49

X-craft 137, 138

Yeovil85
York, Susannah 88
Yorkshire Dales 91
Yugoslavia 82

Zemke, Hubert, Colonel 143, 144, 145
Zemke's *Oregon's Britannia* 143
'Zemke's Wolf Pack' 143, 144